Plato's Republic
A Biography

Other titles in the Books That Shook the World series:
Available now:

Darwin's *Origin of Species* by Janet Browne

Thomas Paine's *Rights of Man* by Christopher Hitchens

The Qur'an by Bruce Lawrence

Marx's *Das Kapital* by Francis Wheen

Adam Smith's *Wealth of Nations* by P. J. O'Rourke

Forthcoming:

The Bible by Karen Armstrong

Homer's *The Iliad and the Odyssey* by Alberto Manguel

Clausewitz's *On War* by Hew Strachan

Machiavelli's *The Prince* by Philip Bobbitt

Plato's
Republic

A Biography

SIMON BLACKBURN

Douglas & McIntyre

VANCOUVER/TORONTO

07 08 09 10 11   5 4 3 2 1

Originated in Great Britain by Atlantic Books, an imprint of Grove Atlantic Ltd.

Published in Canada in 2007 by

Douglas & McIntyre Ltd.
2323 Quebec Street, Suite 201
Vancouver, British Columbia
Canada v5t 4s7
www.douglas-mcintyre.com

Library and Archives Canada Cataloguing in Publication
Blackburn, Simon
Plato's republic: a biography / Simon Blackburn.

(Books that shook the world)
Includes bibliographical references and index.
ISBN 978-1-55365-265-6

1. Plato. Republic. 2. Political science—Philosophy.
I. Title. II. Series: Books that shook the world (Vancouver, B.C.)

JC71.P6B53 2007   321'.07   C2006-906442-3

Jacket design by Peter Dyer
Jacket image courtesy of Getty Images
Interior design by Richard Marston
Printed and bound in Canada by Friesens
Printed on acid-free paper that is forest friendly
(100% post-consumer recycled paper)
and has been processed chlorine free

CONTENTS

I cannot say that this was a book I had been waiting to write. In fact, when I was approached with the prospect, my immediate instinct was to feel flattered, but to decline gracefully. As I explain further in the Introduction, I am neither a classicist nor a historian, even of the amateur variety. And worse than that, if in the present context there can be anything worse than that, I had never felt Plato to be a particularly congenial author. In some respects, as may be apparent from the book, I still do not. On the other hand, it is not really good enough for a philosopher to confess to a Plato-sized blindspot. He is too important, and too entrenched in the Western (and Islamic) tradition to ignore. The question has to be how we are to come to terms with him. Readers wanting to spoil the plot and skip to my own response to that, may read the last sentence of the book.

While I was dithering, I had the good luck to mention the invitation to a friend, the fine classical philosopher Julia Annas, whose own work on Plato infuses this book more than may be apparent. To my surprise, instead of laughing her head off, as she well might have, she immediately offered guidelines and support, even copying various papers and pieces of secondary literature for me herself. This great generosity made me think that perhaps the project was possible after all. Further reading, although filling me with dread at the sheer quantity of classical scholarship that has accumulated over the ages, also suggested that *Republic* has sustained, and still sustains, a wealth of philosophy, politics, and ethics about which one ought to have something to say. So I began to see how interesting the challenge might be, and of course once that idea has taken hold, the rest follows.

I suppose Julia did not singlehandedly conquer my diffidence at entering these unfamiliar waters, or I would have brashly knocked on more distinguished doors here in Cambridge, or in other centres where people who have devoted their lives to Plato are found. No doubt the book would have been better had I done so. But it would also have been longer, and I fear it would have tried the patience of my editor Toby Mundy even more than it has already done, as doubts and difficulties multiplied, turning into delays and rewrites, potentially without end. As it is, apart from gratefully receiving help from Paul Cartledge over Thucydides, I read what I could in Plato with mounting excitement, and before that could begin to cool, wrote the essay without any more ado.

It follows that my principal debts are to my agent, Catherine Clarke, who adroitly managed the initial flattery, and to Julia Annas for the confidence necessary to get started. Alice Hunt read the first draft with exemplary care, and suggested many improvements that I have tried to incorporate. I owe thanks to the University of Cambridge and to Trinity College for a period of sabbatical leave during which the work was done, and to my wife and family for putting up with a great deal of silence, abstraction and sheer exasperation, while I fought, as generations before me have done, with the greatest and most fertile single book of the Western philosophical canon.

Simon Blackburn

Cambridge

Spring 2006

A NOTE ON TRANSLATIONS
AND EDITIONS

Medieval writers knew Plato through translations into Latin, not directly from Greek texts, but from Arabic versions, themselves translated from Greek texts disseminated to Arabic scholars from the Byzantine world. The earliest authoritative translation of Plato to be disseminated in Western Europe was the three-volume Renaissance edition of the scholar Henri Estienne (in Latin, Stephanus), published in Geneva in 1578. It juxtaposed pages of the Greek text of Plato with a Latin translation. From it derives the initially off-putting notation for referring to passages in Plato's works. The numbers, which are printed in the margins in all decent editions, are known as 'Stephanus numbers'. They are page numbers from this edition, followed by letters from a – e referring to sections of the page. The system makes it easy to locate passages without being confined to one or another modern edition or translation. In the present volume I refer to passages in the *Republic* by prefacing the Stephanus number with the number of the Book in question, from I to X, since *Republic* is somewhat arbitrarily divided into ten chapters or 'books'.

Translations of Plato into English were slower to arrive. The first well-known translation from the Greek was that of Thomas Taylor and Floyer Sydenham, published in London in 1804. This was the edition that would have been known to Coleridge and the Romantics. Unfortunately, James Mill (John Stuart's father) said of Thomas Taylor that 'he has not translated Plato; he has travestied him, in the most cruel and abominable manner. He has not elucidated, but covered him over with impenetrable darkness'.

The Victorian interest in Plato produced a translation by Davis and Vaughan, in 1858, and the classic edition by Benjamin Jowett, still one of the most widely disseminated English versions of the dialogues, first published by Oxford University Press in 1871. However, classical scholars are hard to please in these matters, and the exacting scholar A. E. Housman is reported to have described Jowett's as 'the best translation of a Greek philosopher which has ever been executed by a person who understood neither philosophy nor Greek'. Other scholars have not been daunted by the risk of such a reception, and Jowett was followed by Desmond Lee, Francis Cornford, Paul Shorey, I. A. Richards (into basic English), A. D. Lindsay, Allan Bloom, and many others down to the present day. The World's Classics edition by Robin Waterfield that I have used is clear and straightforward, and has excellent notes.

INTRODUCTION

*The safest general characterization of the European philosophical
tradition is that it consists of a series of footnotes to Plato. I do
not mean the systematic scheme of thought which scholars have
doubtfully extracted from his writings. I allude to the wealth of
general ideas scattered through them.*

Alfred North Whitehead, *Process and Reality* (1929)

Before discussing how *Republic* shook the world, we might
ask whether any book shakes the world. Certainly the world
changes, and many of its important changes can be plotted
using the rise and fall of those ideas by which people live:
ideas like freedom and democracy, or justice, citizenship or
knowledge. Religions shake the world, and in practice a religion is just a fossilized philosophy – a philosophy with the
questioning spirit suppressed. Still, there are people who
would say that even if changes in the world can be charted
through ideas, such as those of *Republic*, Plato will not have
been responsible for the changes themselves. The philosopher
merely follows the parade: 'When philosophy paints its grey
in grey, then has a shape of life grown old. The owl of

Minerva spreads its wings only with the coming of the dusk.'[1] Ideas are only the whistle on the engine. What shakes the world are time and circumstance, land, food, guns and money, the economic and social forces that determine the organization of peoples at different times and places.

The author of ideas, on such a view, does not make history but merely receives a larger part in its description. Fortunately we need not investigate what truth there is in this, although it seems unlikely that ideas are as inert as all that, so that nobody is ever changed by reading either *Republic* or any other work of religion, morals or politics, including those very works by Hegel (such as *The Philosophy of History*, 1826) and Marx (such as *The German Ideology*, 1846) in which the idea of the futility of ideas has been suggested. Ideas work on minds. That, after all, is what they are for: we could not be adapted for thought if it was useless. An idea is just a staging post to action. And, although people who pride themselves on their hard-headed 'scientific' approach to human life often find it hard to understand, when we say that ideas (and culture) change things, we are not denying that food and land, guns and money change things. We are not positing some airy-fairy, supernatural force, a 'spirit of the age' hovering somewhere above the more mundane world. We are talking only of the modes in which people think about themselves and their doings, and it is those ways of thinking that, among other things, help to determine who has the land and the food, who picks up the guns, and where the money gets spent.

If any books change the world, *Republic* has a good claim

to first place. The philosopher and mathematician Alfred North Whitehead, quoted at the head of this Introduction, is far from alone in his estimate of Plato's influence. A century earlier the wordy essayist Ralph Waldo Emerson outdid Whitehead in wonder at Plato's genius, in one of the rare pararagraphs worth quoting in full:

> Plato is philosophy, and philosophy, Plato, – at once the glory and the shame of mankind, since neither Saxon nor Roman have availed to add any idea to his categories. No wife, no children had he, and the thinkers of all civilized nations are his posterity, and are tinged with his mind. How many great men Nature is incessantly sending up out of night, to be his men, – Platonist! The Alexandrians, a constellation of genius; the Elizabethans, not less; Sir Thomas More, Henry More, John Hales, John Smith, Lord Bacon, Jeremy Taylor, Ralph Cudworth, Sydenham, Thomas Taylor; Marcilius Ficinus, and Picus Mirandola. Calvinism is in his Phaedo: Christianity is in it. Mahometanism draws all its philosophy, in its hand-book of morals, the Akhlak-y-Jalaly, from him. Mysticism finds in Plato all its texts. This citizen of a town in Greece is no villager nor patriot. An Englishman reads and says, 'how English!' a German – 'how Teutonic!' an Italian – 'how Roman and how Greek!' As they say that Helen of Argos had that universal beauty that everybody felt related to her, so Plato seems, to a reader in New England, an American genius. His broad humanity transcends all sectional lines.[2]

Emerson was himself an illustration of the influence he is describing: his philosophy, known as New England Transcendentalism, blended a heady, Romantic, cult of personality, with a vague assurance of a Higher Order in Things which is itself derived from Platonism.

Nevertheless, Whitehead's famous remark is wrong as it stands. Much of the European tradition in philosophy contains vehement rejections of Plato, rather than footnotes to him. We can scarcely hold that the great materialist and scientific philosophers, from Bacon and Hobbes through Locke, to Hume and Nietzsche simply write footnotes to the Plato they regarded as the fountain of error. So if we want the safety Whitehead proposes, then it is safest to hedge, and to keep only the important germ of truth that the European (and Byzantine and Arabic) philosophical traditions at least consist of a series of responses to Plato. Even those who reject what they associate with Plato are often reacting to him, and often overshadowed by him. And there will be others to tell them that their rejection misfires, and that it was anticipated by Plato himself, or only results from misreading, misunderstanding and simplifying the master.

Such defences are not, as they might seem to be, mere special pleading on behalf of a favourite authority. Plato wrote his philosophy in dialogues, a form which requires different voices, and the ebb and flow of argument. It was already noted back in antiquity that the Socrates who is the hero of these dialogues, and Plato himself, are shifting, mobile figures, readily admitting different interpretations: 'It is well known that Socrates was in the habit of concealing his knowledge, or his beliefs; and Plato approved of the habit', said St Augustine.[3] One way of taking this is that Plato, and presumably Socrates, really did have doctrines to teach, but that for some irritating reason they preferred to unveil them only partially, one bit at a time, in a kind of intellectual strip-tease. This line has occasionally been taken by weak-minded commentators in love with the idea of hidden, esoteric mysteries penetrated only by initiates, among whom they are pleased to imagine themselves. We talk of Leo Strauss's version of the approach later.

But the right way of interpreting Augustine's remark is that Plato felt that philosophy was more a matter of an activity than one of absorbing or learning a static body of doctrine. It is a question of process not product. Socrates remains the great educator, and those who came to him would be listeners and interrogators, participants in conversation, and would have to throw themselves actively into the labyrinths of thought. Passive reception of the word would count for nothing – this was one of the mistakes made by Plato's opponents, the sophists, who charged fees for imparting what they sold as practical wisdom (one might think of the witless piles of 'wisdom' and 'self-help' literature which now choke bookshops).[4] At the end of Plato's dialogue *Phaedrus* Socrates himself makes a speech despising reading philosophy as a poor second to doing it. Many people have made the same point subsequently. Schopenhauer describes reading as a mere surrogate for thinking for yourself, and in turn quotes the German polymath Goethe, 'what you have inherited from your forefathers you must first win for yourself if you are to possess it'.[5]

The important contrast is not so much between reading and listening, but between passive reception and repetition, rote learning, and active thinking for yourself. Whether the engagement is with written or spoken words need not matter, but Plato is right that there are dangers in the written word which the activities of dispute and conversation avoid. The written word is easily turned into an object of recitation or fetish, the foodstuff of unintelligent fundamentalisms. The writer Robert Louis Stevenson put it forcibly, arguing that literature is but the shadow of good talk. 'Talk is fluid, tentative, continually in further search and progress; while written words remain fixed, become idols even to the writer, found wooden dogmatisms, and preserve flies of obvious error in the amber of the truth.'[6]

The insistence on engagement chimes with Plato's adoption of the dialogue form, in which different voices get a hearing, and it is the twists and turns of the processes of argument rather than any set conclusion that help us to expand our minds as we read. Philosophy, in this view, is about discovering things in dialogue and argument ('dialectically'); anything read later could at best be a reminder of the understanding achieved in this process.[7]

This dramatic conception of what Plato is about makes him harder to criticize. One can reject a conclusion, but it is much harder to reject a process of imaginative expansion, and if we take the link with drama seriously, it might seem as silly as 'rejecting' *King Lear* or *Hamlet*. But in fact the parallel does not cut off criticism, but encourages it. For in the course of Plato's dramas theses do get stated and defended, arguments are made, and people are persuaded. This is the kind of dramas they are. Sometimes the drama comes to an end with an apparent conclusion – after all, the thesis about the superiority of dialectical activity to passive exposure such as reading allows is itself one of them.[8] And in all these cases it is appropriate to ask whether the theses, arguments and conclusions are in fact acceptable. Doing this is doing no more than taking part in the drama or entering the dialectical arena, the very activity that Socrates and Plato commend. And this is particularly so with *Republic*, which is far from a light game of tennis with ideas, none of which are seriously entertained. It is impossible to read it without again and again feeling that we are confronting deep and serious doctrines. It is of little importance, except to biographers, whether these are Plato's own doctrines. They are there in the book, and for philosophy and history, that is enough.[9]

Republic is commonly regarded as the culminating achievement of Plato as a philosopher and writer, brilliantly poised between the questioning and inconclusive earlier dialogues, and the less compelling cosmological speculations, and doubts, of the later ones. Over the centuries it has probably sustained more commentary, and been subject to more radical and impassioned disagreement, than almost any other of the great founding texts of the modern world. Indeed, the history of readings of the book is itself an academic discipline, with specialist chapters on almost every episode in the story of religion and literature for the last two thousand years and more. To take only the major English poets, there are entire distinct books on Platonism and Chaucer, Spenser, Shakespeare, Milton, Blake, Shelley and Coleridge, to name but a few, and of course there are many others on whole movements and times: Plato and Christianity, Plato and the Renaissance, Plato and the Victorians, Plato and the Nazis, Plato and us.[10] The story of Plato's direct influence on philosophy is another study in itself, and one peppered with names that are better known to specialists than to the world at large: Philo Judaeus, Macrobius, Porphyry, Pseudo-Dionysius, Eriugena, as well as the better-known Plotinus, Augustine or Dante. Sometimes the Plato in question is the author of other texts, notably the inspirational dialogue *Symposium* and the theologically ambitious *Timaeus*. But *Republic* is seldom far away.

Anyone who stays very long in the vast silent mausoleums lined with works about Plato and his influence runs the risk of suffocating. Anyone writing on this topic must be conscious of an enormous and disapproving audience, dizzying ranks of ghosts overseeing and criticizing omissions and simplifications. Many of these ghosts belong to the most brilliant linguists, scholars, philosophers, theologians and historians of their day. They do not take kindly to the garden to which they devoted their lives being trampled over by outsiders and infidels. And *Republic* is the shrine at the very centre of the sanctuary, since for centuries it has been the one compulsory subject in the philosophy syllabus, so these same scholars will have been educated with it as the centrepiece and inspiration. Nor is this attention merely historical: a distinguished modern Platonist says, rightly, that the sun never sets on the reading of Plato: 'always, someone somewhere is reading the *Republic*'.[11]

But as I have said, Plato and his *Republic* have their detractors, and we might initially find all this attention incomprehensible. In Raphael's famous painting in the Vatican, known as *The School of Athens*, Plato and Aristotle together hold centre-stage, but while Aristotle points to the earth, Plato points upwards to the Heavens.[12]

The poet Coleridge made the same contrast, saying that everyone was born either a Platonist or an Aristotelian, meaning that Plato is otherworldly, a dealer in abstractions, while Aristotle is the plain empirical man who faces things as they are in the world as we find it. Coleridge continued that 'I don't think it possible that any one born an Aristotelian *can* become a Platonist, and I am sure no born Platonist *can* ever change into an Aristotelian.'[13] In this opposition, Aristotle represents what George W. Bush's White House referred to contemptuously as the 'reality-based community', which believes that 'solutions emerge from the judicious study of discernible reality'. Plato is the patron saint of ascent away from the reality-based community. In his own time the Athenian comic playwright Aristophanes satirized Plato's hero Socrates by placing him among the clouds.

If these are the options, then one might expect the minds of the reality-based community, focused upon experience, to prove fitter than those that take themselves off to cloud-cuckoo land. In a Darwinian world, we might expect the former eventually to oust the latter altogether. Dreaming is of little use, while coming to grips with the way of things surely is. And ours is a practical, scientific, empirical civilization, which provides an inhospitable climate to dreamers. It is surprising, then, that Plato is not more neglected, and we may wonder whether his appeal is the result of a conspiracy between dry-as-dust scholars and mad visionaries and theologians.

Such was the view of Francis Bacon, the great proponent of the scientific revolution at the beginning of the seventeenth century. One of Bacon's concerns was the just basis of scientific taxonomies, or the sorting of things into manageable kinds, in a world with no chemistry, no accurate mechanics, and little botany or biology, and he grudgingly allows Plato some credit for the Socratic insistence on definition and accurate meaning. But more generally he saw Plato, along with other Greek philosophers, as a leading example of the mind's 'premature and precipitate haste', a sophist himself but even more dangerous:

> The disputatious and *sophistical* kind of philosophy catches the understanding in a trap, but the other kind, the fantastic, high-blown, semi-poetical philosophy seduces it. There is in man a kind of ambition of the intellect no less than of the will, especially in lofty, high-minded characters. A conspicuous

example of this occurs among the Greeks in Pythagoras, where it is combined with a rather crass and cumbrous *superstition*, and in a more perilous and subtle form in Plato and his school...[14]

Greek philosophy in general, thought Bacon, deserved the response reported to have been made by Dionysius I, the tyrant of Syracuse: 'the words of idle old men to callow youths'. Such, as well, was the stout eighteenth-century reaction to Plato, expressed by the forthright Alexander Pope:

> Go, soar with Plato to th'empyreal sphere,
> To the first good, first perfect, and first fair;
> Or tread the mazy round his followers trod,
> And quitting sense call imitating God;[15]

'Quitting sense' here is nicely ambiguous: both abandoning, or pretending to transcend, the ordinary world as we experience it, and (as a result) entering realms of religion-flavoured nonsense. This was the standard eighteenth-century view. Even the acute and generous sage of the Scottish Enlightenment, David Hume, faltered when it came to representing the character of the Platonist, being able to manage no more than a caricature or pastiche of life spent in rapturous contemplation of Divine and Eternal Things, or perhaps the one Divine and Eternal Thing.[16]

One of the most forceful rejections of Plato comes from the historian and essayist Lord Macaulay, writing yet later, in 1837, when the Victorian adoption of Plato was just getting under way:

Assuredly if the tree which Socrates planted and Plato watered is to be judged of by its flowers and leaves, it is the noblest of trees. But if we take the homely test of Bacon, if we judge of the tree by its fruits, our opinion of it may perhaps be less favourable. When we sum up all the useful truths which we owe to that philosophy, to what do they amount? We find, indeed, abundant proofs that some of those who cultivated it were men of the first order of intellect. We find among their writings incomparable specimens both of dialectical and rhetorical art. We have no doubt that the ancient controversies were of use, in so far as they served to exercise the faculties of the disputants; for there is no controversy so idle that it may not be of use in this way. But, when we look for something more, for something which adds to the comforts or alleviates the calamities of the human race, we are forced to own ourselves disappointed. We are forced to say with Bacon that this celebrated philosophy ended in nothing but disputation, that it was neither a vineyard nor an olive-ground, but an intricate wood of briars and thistles, from which those who lost themselves in it brought back many scratches and no food.[17]

The otherworldly Plato is certainly supposed to make his appearance in *Republic*. Part of its fascination is the cleavage between the relatively practical programme of moral and political education, and the mystical gloss on it somewhat rhapsodically voiced in the centre of the work. In those sections Plato certainly appears to downgrade the world of matter, the world of sense, as a mere world of shadows. The path of wisdom leads us away from concern with that world. By contrast there is a world of final, immutable, changeless objects of contemplation, at the summit of which stands the ultimate object of a special kind of knowledge independent of sense experience. This is also the ultimately real and the ultimately fitting object of love and desire: a constantly radiant eternal source of light, the form of the good itself. This is his 'transcendental' streak – meaning an interest in subject matters and ways of knowing beyond the empirical world, and beyond our access to it by means of sense experience. As we shall see, the interpretation of his idea of ascent is much contested, but however it falls out, Plato, like many theologians, would indignantly insist on his place in the reality-based community. It is just that the reality in which he is based is higher, better, beyond our everyday world of shadows and illusions, fixed and eternal – really real.

Religious Platonism is described by Aldous Huxley in terms of 'the perennial philosophy', in his book of that name:

the metaphysic that recognizes a divine Reality substantial to the world of things and lives and minds; the psychology that finds in the soul something similar to, or even identical with, divine Reality; the ethic that places man's final end in the knowledge of the immanent and transcendent Ground of all being – the thing is immemorial and universal. Rudiments of the Perennial Philosophy may be found among the traditional lore of primitive peoples in every region of the world, and in its fully developed forms it has a place in every one of the higher religions[18]

We may or may not find ourselves enchanted by the vision of a metaphysical ascent, depending on whether we were born Platonists or Aristotelians. Our point at present is that while it makes Plato a religious inspiration, it ought to have made him rebarbative to those of a more empirical bent, and as I have been detailing, it has fairly often done so. Yet *Republic* has been not only an inspiration to poets and mystics, but the trusted companion of educators and reformers, and men with their finger firmly on the pulse of government and current affairs, such as John Stuart Mill or Shelley himself (whose poetry was firmly in the service of political reform) or that pillar of Victorian earnestness, the renowned Master of Balliol, Benjamin Jowett.[19]

Part of the solution may be that the otherworldly theme is more prominent in other dialogues, such as the *Timaeus* and the *Phaedo*. It was the first of these especially that came down through antiquity to influence Christian thought, the Neoplatonists of the third century AD, St Augustine, Boethius, the Renaissance Platonists, and for that matter Coleridge himself. One can ignore the metaphysical ambition for large parts of *Republic*, reading the work as Plato-lite, as it were. There is still a visionary quality about it, but then only in the sense that it promotes an ideal or image of what a better social world, or a better person, would be like. In that sense, almost any work of moral and political philosophy, from the

Upanishads to the New Testament to Marx, is visionary. And the contrast with Aristotle breaks down, for he too has his ideals and his recipes for the good life. Aristotle himself spent some twenty years as a member of Plato's circle in Athens, which scarcely suggests disaffection root and branch.

Much of *Republic* can be read as Plato-lite. These parts can be read regardless of our attitude to the heavy-duty metaphysics of the central chapters, although we have to wrestle with Huxley's perennial philosophy in due course, when we come to those central parts, and notably the part that everyone remembers, the Myth of the Cave. I shall argue that on its best interpretation, it is far from suggesting an airy-fairy, visionary picture of divine raptures and illuminations. In fact, we can tame it, and see it as no more than a sensible plea for just the kind of understanding of the actual world that science and mathematics offer us now, two millennia later. Perhaps Plato has been horribly betrayed by Platonists – not an uncommon fate for a great philosopher.

But there are other less doctrinal reasons why the sovereignty of *Republic* ought to be surprising. The work is long, sprawling and meandering. We shall find that far from holding water its arguments range from ordinarily leaky to leaky in that special, zany way that leaves some interpreters unable to recognize them as ever intended to hold water at all. Its apparent theory of human nature is fanciful, and might seem inconsistent. Its apparent political implications are mainly disagreeable, and often appalling. We should not mince words: in so far as Plato has a legacy in politics, it includes theocracy or rule by priests, militarism, nationalism, hierarchy, illiberalism, totalitarianism, and the complete disdain of the economic structures of society, born in his case of privileged slave-ownership. In *Republic* he managed simultaneously to attach himself both to the most static conservatism and to the most wild-eyed utopianism. On top of all that, the book's theory of knowledge is a disaster. Its attempt to do what it apparently sets out to do, which is to show that the moral individual, and only the moral individual, is happy, is largely a sequence of conjuring tricks.

More insidiously, in so far as there is now an aesthetic tone associated with Plato, it is not one to which we easily succumb, unless we have absorbed too much of it to escape. Plato's high summer, in England at least, lay in the golden glow of the late Victorian and Edwardian age – the vaguely homoerotic, vaguely religious, emotionally arrested, leisured, class-conscious world of playing fields, expensive schools and lazy universities, the world of Walter Pater, or E. M. Forster, of half-forgotten belletrists and aesthetes like John Addington Symonds or Goldsworthy Lowes Dickinson, or golden boy-poets like Rupert Brooke. This is not the world around us. It is not quite a world of slave-ownership, but capitalism throws up its own drones.

An equally shocking thing about it in some people's eyes is that in writing *Republic* Plato utterly betrayed his teacher Socrates. Socrates is the first and greatest liberal hero and martyr to freedom in thought and speech. For writers like John Stuart Mill and George Grote – practical, liberal, utilitarian thinkers – this was the real Socrates, the eternal spirit of reflection, criticism and potentially of opposition to the state itself. But in *Republic* he is presented as an out-and-out dogmatist, rather than the open-minded, patient, questioning spirit his admirers love. He is shown as the spokesman for a repressive, authoritarian, static, hierarchical society in which everything up to and including sexual relations and birth control is regulated by the political classes, who deliberately use lies for the purpose. He presents a social system in which the liberal Socrates would have been executed a great deal more promptly than he was by the Athenian democracy. In *Republic* the liberal Socrates has become the spokesman for a dictatorship. In presenting this figure Plato even betrayed his own calling, being once a poet, who now calls for the poets to be banned.

A work may have many defects, yet be forgiven if the author comes through as a creature of sweetness and light, just as Plato's literary creation, the Socrates of the earlier dialogues, does. But there is not much help here. True, there must have been enough sweetness and light in Plato to create the figure of the heroic, liberal Socrates in the first place. But if that figure evaporates, as it does in *Republic*, there is not much else to go into the balance. We know very little about Plato, and what there is to know is not generally appealing. If he is put in historical context, we may find an archetypal grumpy old man, a disenchanted aristocrat, hating the Athenian democracy, convinced that the wrong people are in charge, with a deep fear of democracy itself, constantly sneering at artisans, farmers, and indeed all productive labour, deeply contemptuous of any workers' ambition for education, and finally manifesting an immature hankering after the appalling military despotism of Sparta.

But as so often with Plato, there is a complication to that picture, nicely brought out in Friedrich Nietzsche's pleased reaction to the delightful fact that on Plato's deathbed he turned out to have been reading the comic writer Aristophanes (who was also a friend):

> there is nothing that has caused me to meditate more on Plato's secrecy and sphinx-like nature, than the happily preserved *petit fait* [little fact] that under the pillow of his deathbed there was found no 'Bible', nor anything Egyptian, Pythagorean, or Platonic – but a book of Aristophanes. How could even Plato have endured life – a Greek life which he repudiated – without an Aristophanes?[20]

We are told that Jesus wept, but not that he ever laughed. With Plato, as with Socrates, laughter is often nearer than it seems. This is a good sign. Perhaps the grumpy old man was not quite so grumpy after all. But this does not really matter, for it is the concrete, enduring book that concerns us, not its shadowy and departed author. And it is a good dictum that while many books are wrongly forgotten, no book is wrongly remembered. So we need to work harder to come to terms with the unquestioned staying power of *Republic*. We need to understand something of the hold this book has had and continues to have on the imagination of readers. What follows is a modest attempt at that task.

It is written, as is perhaps already apparent, by a natural sceptic. My temperament is irreligious and empiricist, down with Aristotle and the reality-based community, rather than up with Platonism in the heavens. When at the beginning of my philosophical life I came across Plato's dialogues, I was far from enchanted, even by the earlier, less dogmatic ones. I could see that the figure of Socrates had a certain charm, but only up to a point, as his relentless grindings put me in mind of nothing more than some dreadful lawyer bent on confusing any poor victim in his clutches. I could respond to his rhetoric, rising to something sublime when, for instance, in the *Crito*, he defends his submission to the unjust verdict of the city of Athens that condemned him to death. But even here the heroism grated a little, striking me in some moods as a kitsch reduction to absurdity of classical virtue.

I saw Plato's arguments themselves as often little more than cheap point-scoring, and certainly no better than the material that he puts in the mouth of his professed opponents, the sophists. Worse than that, I saw his whole picture of the soul's ascent as a reactionary, primitive, useless obstacle to the path of real understanding, which lies in science. Plato, together with his vulgarization in Christianity, was something that had to be overcome in order for the Enlightenment to win. So it is not in a spirit of piety that I enter on this slight essay.

But I would plead that this distance is a kind of qualification for what I am attempting. True, it means I have little conscience about skipping over tracts of discussion that still strike me as profitless, where more sympathetic or more patient interpreters strain every nerve to extract some real or imagined good from them. Perhaps my best defence is that if even someone like myself could come to understand the overwhelming intellectual or moral or spiritual force that history has allowed to Plato, then I might be well placed to enable others to follow, more so than if I had started even partly willing to let myself get carried away.

This mind-set also explains something about the architecture of the book. I had originally planned a run-through of the highlights of *Republic*, followed by an essay in the history of ideas, saying something about how later cultures and later thinkers responded to it. This plan foundered, because I am neither a classicist nor a historian by training. I find it easy to tiptoe past large tracts of history, here at least following the distinguished early twentieth-century Platonist Paul Shorey:

> We need not recur to the Middle Ages further than to add one example of medieval confusion of thought and of the way in which the *Timaeus* of Plato exalted their imaginations and confounded their ideas.[21]

Like Shorey, I find I can sidle past quite a lot of the history of Platonism, with nothing but a sigh of relief.

Indeed, I can congratulate myself on being unusually free of what Bertrand Russell called the evil of specialization, which dictates that 'a man must not write on Plato unless he has spent so much of his youth on Greek as to have had no time for the things Plato thought important'.[22] This means that my instinct is to home in on the ideas themselves, rather than on Plato's own context as he writes them down, and still less on whatever Cicero or Augustine or King Alfred or John Stuart Mill made of them. Instead, I have freely mingled presenting the plot of the book, the historical residues and responses, and something of the cultural worlds that Plato helped to shape. Perhaps this means that I am not writing a biography of the book, and certainly I am not writing a history of the life of *Republic*, so much as a case-study of it, but I suppose that too is a kind of biography. So Plato himself, Christianity, seventeenth-century writers like Locke or Hobbes, nineteenth-century ones like Nietzsche, twenty-first century neo-conservatives and many others can find themselves cheek by jowl in any section. Perhaps the chapters to come are best read only as a preparation for a biography of the book, telling us just a little of why its life has been so long and so distinguished.

CHAPTER 1

Convention and Amoralism

What is at stake is far from insignificant: it is how one should live one's life. (I, 352d)

Republic was probably written around 375 BC, when Plato was in his early fifties (he was born as an Athenian aristocrat around 428 BC and died in 347 BC). It is conventionally divided into ten books, although there is no reason to think that this organization was Plato's own: it derives from the arbitrary length of an ancient papyrus rather than from any argumentative rhythm. It is common to regard the first book as something of an introduction, and the last book as something of a coda or endpiece, but they are both important, dramatically and doctrinally. The central discussion of morality and politics, however, runs through Books II to IX. Within it, there is a substantial subsidiary part, Books V to VII, which concern other parts of philosophy as well, notably the theory of knowledge, and the nature of reality (epistemology and metaphysics). These three central books are where the metaphysical temperature rises. They contain some of Plato's most famous and radical doctrines, including the notorious defence of the philosopher-kings, and the famous Myth of the Cave. In so far as *Republic* has a metaphysical heartland, this is where it lies.

The leading character is of course Socrates. The historical Socrates had been executed by the Athenian democracy, in 399 BC, some twenty-five years before *Republic* was written, for the crime that he did not acknowledge duly the gods that the city acknowledged, invented new unacknowledged divinities, and corrupted the young. It is therefore a significant touch that the drama starts when Socrates piously goes down to the port of Piraeus, just outside the city of Athens, to pray, however, at a new festival, to an imported goddess. There is also a telling dramatic contrast with the dialogue *The Symposium*, which concerns the ascent of the soul, and begins with a journey up to the city rather than down from it. The first leitmotif, that of the uneasy relation between piety and criticism, between the customary usages of the city and the restless spirit of examination, is immediately established.

Not only is this the first leitmotif, but it sounds throughout *Republic*, throughout many of Plato's other dialogues, and it echoes down the centuries to our own time. It confronts us with a choice. Is there nothing to living well except conformity to customary usage? Or is there also a possibility of a critical standpoint, a kind of external rationale to some particular set of rules or laws, such as, ideally, a proof that they deserve allegiance or that they alone provide a rational way of life for human beings? Is it a matter of simply conforming to whichever rules happen to be in place, in order to play the social game or is there something more, capable of underwriting the authority of those rules? Writing perhaps sixty or seventy years before Plato, the historian Herodotus noticed the overwhelming place of custom in people's minds:

> For if one were to offer men to choose out of all the customs in the world such as seemed to them the best, they would examine the whole number, and end by preferring their own; so convinced are they that their own usages far surpass those of all others… Such is men's wont herein; and Pindar was right, in my judgment, when he said, 'Law is the king o'er all'.[1]

Custom, or *nomos* in the sense Herodotus is quoting from the poet Pindar, embraces the rules of the community, the conventional system of norms enforced by the mutual watchfulness of a group. Jumping to the end of the seventeenth century, it is what John Locke called the 'law of fashion' and is enforced by fear of reputation and ambition for esteem:

> Thus the measure of what is everywhere called and esteemed virtue and vice is this approbation or dislike, praise or blame, which, by a secret and tacit consent, establishes itself in the several societies, tribes, and clubs of men in the world: whereby several actions come to find credit or disgrace amongst them, according to the judgment, maxims, or fashion of that place… But no man escapes the punishment of their censure and dislike, who offends against the fashion and

opinion of the company he keeps, and would recommend himself to. Nor is there one of ten thousand, who is stiff and insensible enough, to bear up under the constant dislike and condemnation of his own club. He must be of a strange and unusual constitution, who can content himself to live in constant disgrace and disrepute with his own particular society.[2]

Plato is well aware of the attractions of going no further than this. Indeed, one of the most eloquent set speeches in any dialogue, the so-called 'great speech' from *Protagoras*, argues that we need nothing more.[3] In it Protagoras (one of the disdained sophists) in effect gives an evolutionary psychology of morality, just by regarding it in this light, and showing how it enables men to cooperate and coordinate their actions, and thereby fulfil their mutual needs. The 'law of fashion' is therefore not just something slightly shameful that we happen to go in for, as it were, out of a desire for popularity, or for fitting in with the gang. It is a natural and essential expression of human nature and human need. Our responsiveness to the law of fashion is a matter of internalizing the voices of others, as they would be poised to praise or condemn whatever we are doing. We absorb it, as it were by contagion, as a motive of our own, inclining us for or against a course of action. This responsiveness is a Darwinian adaptation, for human life with it will be more successful than life without it. In this area, we are all clubmen, all fashionistas.

The view that morality is in this sense the law of fashion is probably the dominant contemporary view of ethics, both among philosophers thinking of themselves as scientific in outlook, and especially amongst psychologists and evolutionary theorists. It can be served in different flavours. Locke, for instance, seemed to have in mind the way we absorb the opinion of other contemporaries. A particular variation of the type would be the touchy 'man of honour', whom we consider later. A variation might stress parental pressure, and more lurid Freudian variations might speculate about the psychological stresses involved in infancy as we resist having our wills moulded by outside forces. But whichever way we elaborate it, Plato regards it with suspicion and hostility.

This suspicion and hostility is shared, on different grounds, by classical liberalism. The fear is the tyranny of custom: the stifling, conservative, unthinking pressure of 'the done thing' or 'good form' or tradition. George Grote, the great Victorian historian and philosopher, a friend of Mill and liberal member of Parliament, talked with particular dislike of the rule of custom, Pindar's *nomos basileus* or what he christened King Nomos, and whose tyranny was enforced by 'the working of that spontaneous ever-present police by whom the authority of King Nomos is enforced in detail – a police not the less omnipotent because they wear no uniform, and carry no recognized title'.[4]

But King Nomos has his defenders. In contemporary times 'communitarians' stress the implicit wisdom in inherited folkways. They may, like the eighteenth-century conservative thinker and parliamentarian Edmund Burke, hold that freedom from King Nomos is neither desirable, nor possible.[5] It is not possible because we are the kinds of animals already sketched. We only gain our self-identity through the gaze of others. And it is not desirable because a 'rational' substitute – such as a scheme of civil society dreamed up on the drawing board – is infinitely less likely to work than one that has stood the test of time, insensibly and gradually adapting itself to the circumstances of living. We shall find that Plato is no fan of liberalism. But he cannot side with Burke, for he is himself centrally in the business of reason. His whole project can be seen as one of thinking morality through from first principles, and of dreaming up schemes on the drawing board.

The opposition between the hope for a 'rational founda-tion' for ethics, and contentment with nothing beyond a foun-dation in custom and convention, is one of philosophy's great divides. For many, it is painful and vertiginous to suppose that their cherished values stand on nothing firmer than custom and convention. It strips our favourite commitments of the dignities of reason, and substitutes the possibly invisible chains of culture: mere ideology, instead of rational law. But for others there is nothing sceptical or upsetting about confronting the fact that our ways are ultimately nothing more than our ways. In modern philosophy the idea that rules, including moral rules, simply reflect the way we happen to find it natural to go on, has been aided by massive authorities, including two giants of twentieth-

century philosophy, W. V. Quine and Ludwig Wittgenstein. It
fits well with the 'postmodernist' picture of our minds as
largely made up of (and made up by) the forces of convention,
custom and, in the background, power.

Burke wrote in Britain at a time of relative political
complacency and nervous conservatism, against the licence
and upheaval witnessed in the French Revolution. Plato
had a less comfortable historical bed to lie back upon: he
was writing during a long period of Athenian upheaval,
revolution, experiment, war and eventual decline. No
wonder he thought that things needed designing on a more
accurate plan than anything provided by the doodlings of
history. He is certain that the reign of King Nomos is not
good enough.

In *Protagoras* Socrates attempts to rebut the view with
some rather unconvincing logic-chopping. In Book I of
Republic the position is, as it were, spread out in two rich, conservative, self-satisfied tradesmen: Polemarchus and his
father Cephalus. Socrates's conversation with these two men
is inconclusive, at best. In fact, it largely meanders around
some uninteresting swordplay over whether a good man can
ever harm anybody. It also shows Socrates's irritating intel-
lectualism: his tendency to think that if you cannot define
something then you do not know what it is. He shows that
these contented and conventional men cannot do a very good
job of defining virtue. Their initial attempts are at best stum-
bling – but why should that be a problem? The law of fashion
does not have to be articulated in order to work. Nobody can

write down the rules of English grammar, but we can exert sufficient pressure on each other to conform to them. We can recognize what we cannot define.

Ideologically, the opposition between the rule of reason and the rule of custom is sharp enough. However, it can be softened when the conventionalist position is refined in various ways. First, conventions do not have to be accepted just as they are. There can be room for criticism and reflection, itself based on other aspects of convention and custom. In a familiar metaphor, we can stand on some planks of our boat, and repair others. Second, conventions and customs serve purposes, and those purposes assist their authority, and even provide a foundation, only of a different kind. Conventions assist needs and desires, some more important than others. The goals of coordinating with others, of finding peaceful solutions, of communicating, of finding ways of signalling reliability and trust, all enable recognizably human life to go forward. It is not belittling to the authority of promises, any more than it is to the authority of grammar, that it rests on filling such a need. Conventions arise to meet the needs determined by our natures. They are not arbitrary, or rather, it is simplistic and only half the picture to say that they are. It is not arbitrary that we need a convention to determine which side of the road to drive upon. It is only arbitrary how that need is met in detail: whether we find ourselves on the left or the right.

In Aristotle the stark opposition between reason and custom is moderated in another way. There is a threefold support for the idea of law: nature, custom and reason. Nature gives us the purely animal material with which custom or culture, and reason, have to work. Custom or *ethos* arises in the way we have imagined conformities arising, as we coordinate on things like rituals, or on patterns that enable us to cooperate. It transcends nature because it generates a social system of norms which is itself distinct from brute animal habit. Finally, laws, enacted by reason, shape custom. But they cannot exist without it: 'in every case the lower faculty can exist apart from the higher, but the higher presupposes those below it'.[6] As we shall see again in chapter 9, Plato's tendency of mind is to sever the presupposition, thinking, in this area and others, that reason can float free of its earthly and earthy constraints in nature and custom. By contrast, the modern tendency is to think of this 'reason' itself in terms of the political and rhetorical, the give and take of words in parliaments and courts, words which only custom and habit will make weigh with those who find themselves swayed by them (and then get called 'good reasons' for one decision or another). King Nomos rules again.

Of course, Plato remains right to insist on space for criticism, and since he thinks that we have many fewer needs and very different natures than people normally suppose, he will continue to distrust the customs and conventions of any actual time and place. Plato supposes that King Nomos must not be allowed to rule, for disordered communities will have disordered folkways, and will encourage and enforce disordered norms as a result. He is certain that communities can be disordered: in Book VIII he gives a little taxonomy of the various ways this happens (see chapter 14). He scarcely confronts Polemarchus and Cephalus head-on in Book I. Dramatically, however, the inconclusive conversation sets the scene for the explosive entry of another modern figure, not the evolutionary psychologist or the communitarian, not a Wittgenstein or a Foucault with a subtle reinterpretation of the sources of authority, but the impatient, cynical amoralist, one of the first anti-heroes, the intransigent, cynical and sarcastic sophist Thrasymachus.

CHAPTER 2

Might and Right

*My claim is that morality is nothing other than the advantage
of the stronger party… Well, why aren't you applauding?*
(I, 338c)

The historian Thucydides recounts one of the grimmest
episodes of his grim history of the Peloponnesian War, in
which Athens, from a position of power, required the surrender of the tiny independent island state of Melos, in the west
of the group of islands known as the Cyclades. The event
happened in 416–5 BC, some forty years before *Republic*, when
the Athenians sent thirty-eight warships, and some 10,000
men, against the Melians' paltry 500. One can imagine that
Thrasymachus was modelled on one of the implacable and
insolent Athenian envoys to the island. First, these envoys
brutally dismiss appeals to equity or justice and right, and
insist that the case must be argued in terms of self-interest:

> You know as well as we do that right, as the world goes, is
> only in question between equals in power, while the strong
> do what they can and the weak suffer what they must.

The Melians fail to convince Athens that their own best interest lies in a friendly alliance. Why not let them go on being neutral? Because, say the Athenians, we are at war with Sparta, and we have other subjects who need controlling. So you are either for us or against us:

> for your hostility cannot so much hurt us, as your friendship
> will be an argument to our subjects of our weakness, and
> your enmity of our power.

Finally, the Melians turn to the hope that since justice is on their side, they may yet gain the protection of the gods, only to meet this chilling reply:

> When you speak of the favour of the gods, we may as fairly
> hope for that as yourselves; neither our pretensions nor our
> conduct being in any way contrary to what men believe of
> the gods, or practise among themselves. Of the gods we
> believe, and of men we know, that by a necessary law of
> their nature they rule wherever they can. And it is not as if
> we were the first to make this law, or to act upon it when
> made: we found it existing before us, and shall leave it to
> exist for ever after us; all we do is to make use of it, knowing
> that you and everybody else, having the same power as we
> have, would do the same as we do. Thus, as far as the gods
> are concerned, we have no fear and no reason to fear that we
> shall be at a disadvantage.[1]

In Plato's drama, Thrasymachus is in effect the spokesman for the Athenian envoys. They represent the Machiavellian men of realpolitik, knowing they live in a dog-eat-dog world and adapting themselves to it. They and their successors leave a long red stain on human history (the Melians did not surrender, and the Athenians slaughtered the men and enslaved the women and children). They are the direct ancestors of blitzkrieg, terrorism, the worship of the free market, and the ethics of the business school. They are also the direct ancestors of American 'neo-conservatism', the ideology owing its immediate inspiration to political theorist and Plato student Leo Strauss, whom we meet again briefly in chapter 15.

In the nineteenth century Thrasymachus got a boost from the arrival of Darwinism, which was often interpreted as showing that a dog-eat-dog world was not only morally justifiable, but somehow inevitable, so that it was useless to try to moderate it or make any attempt to ease its harsh effects. Realpolitik was nature's own law. Winners win, and losers go to the wall. The logic of unbridled capitalism was nature's own logic, with which it would be not only futile, but impious to tamper. The results of course included poor or non-existent social provision internally, colonialism and imperialism abroad, and competition between the industrialized nations turning to militaristic expansion and aggressive arms races.

The Melian debate shows that Thrasymachus was no straw figure, any more than he was in the nineteenth century or indeed is now, and it will take more than a puff of argument to answer him (it is also worth remembering that before the philosopher Thomas Hobbes became famous for his bleak description of the state of nature as 'the war of all against all', he produced the first English translation of Thucydides from Greek, in 1628).[2]

Thrasymachus is usually presented as challenging Socrates and his talk of morality head-on. But this is not quite right. In one important respect he is an *ally* of Socrates. He reveals the complacency of the 'law of fashion', or, if you like, the relatively bland evolutionary defence of morality represented by Polemarchus and Cephalus. For if morality is in effect nothing more than social glue, the Athenian envoys are right and there is nothing for the Melians to say. Amongst Athenians, the 'credit or reputation' of the envoys is perfectly intact. Their own law of fashion does not condemn them in their own eyes. Acting as trustees of Athens's own interests, they are behaving perfectly rationally. And, they say, they are doing no more than gods and men alike expect. True, it might be added, the Athenians are dissolving any social glue that might have bound their interests up with those of the Melians. But since they are strong and the Melians weak, this is not a social glue they have any interest in fortifying. Their other colonies will be cowed and their empire will be all the stronger if they are seen not to need it, so the friendship of the Melians is actually a handicap.

For many contemporary philosophers, the eighteenth-century German Kant offers us our best hope of arguing against the Athenian envoys. This hope is pinned on the famous 'categorical imperative', the lynchpin of Kantian ethics. Kant argues that breaking promises and telling lies cannot be universalized, because in a world in which it was universal, and known to be so, that one broke a promise or told a lie when it was expedient to do so, there could be no promising and no communication or passing of information, lie or not. The policy is revealed as somehow inconsistent or self-undermining, destroying the foundations that alone make it a possible policy to follow. The success or failure of Kant's approach has been hotly contested ever since he formulated it. But whatever our views on that, the argument is not set to cut much ice with the Athenians, since they not only claim that their stance can be universalized – they claim it is not only possible but actual, already universal, and universal on heaven and earth, among both men and gods. The strong do what they can, and the weak suffer what they must.

Another generalization of the Kantian idea hopes to show that the discipline of reason imposes decency: if the Athenians are to reason with the Melians then the upshot of their reasoning cannot be the victimization or destruction of the Melians themselves. As conversational partners the Melians cannot be expected to agree to this, after all. But the Athenian envoys have several options for replying to this. First, they may ask why they are to care about reasoning with the Melians in the first place. But better, they may reply with some justice that they have just reasoned with the Melians: they have just shown them that by using superior force to compel their submission, the Athenians are not only behaving as gods and men always do, but also as the Melians themselves would if the position were reversed. This may sound like an off-colour reason, perhaps. But it would not sound quite so off-colour if the Melians had behaved the same way on past occasions towards other weaker neighbours. And the Athenians would say that it is only accident whether they have or not, for they are as disposed to behave in such a way as everyone else. The more 'reason' is cranked up to disallow this from counting as a reason, the more the Athenians can ask why reason, in this cranked-up sense, must concern them. And this is enough to show that Kant's approach fails to give us an effective way of articulating our revulsion at the Athenian envoys.

What other resources have we? Aristotelians in moral philosophy try to show that acting virtuously and doing well, or 'flourishing', coincide. And when the social set-up is right – when reputation and advantage and peace of mind all accrue only to the virtuous and never to the rest, they may be right. But they are not on the face of it right about the Athenians, who confidently expect to flourish all the more by killing or enslaving the Melians rather than by leaving them in peace. The dialogue shows that they have made their cost-benefit calculation, and have no doubt which way it tips. They may be right. We could try opposing this by suggesting that they may not sleep easy, may not have clear consciences, and that this will be a brake on their flourishing. In the terms that David Hume, the eighteenth-century Scottish philosopher, used, the mind of a blackguard or villain may not be able to 'bear its own survey'.[3] We might hope this, but it may be a pious hope.

For in principle they can sleep easy, having done their job, or if they cannot, they can say that a bad conscience is after all only a sign of squeamishness, from which they could reasonably wish themselves free.

Thrasymachus did not need to say that morality was the advantage of the stronger party. He could better have said that in so far as it is not, but purports to stand in the way of the stronger party, it is nothing. It gets swept aside, by both gods and men. He does not even have to say that morality is always nothing. Shakespeare's Falstaff says exactly that: 'What is honour? A word. What is that word, honour? Air.'[4] But that is overstating it. Thrasymachus (like Falstaff, and business schools and neo-conservatives) can perfectly well admit that when it is nicely supported by reputation, by the prospect of mutual advantage, and by all the sanctions of King Nomos or the law of fashion, then honour, or justice or equity can motivate people to do the cooperative thing. He can even encourage morality up to a point, arguing that when it comes to internal affairs rather than international relations, since a strong social order requires a docile citizenry, the state is justified in mobilizing propaganda and lies, religious ideology and brain-washing, in order to keep the lower orders jumping through the conventional hoops. What he does need to say is that when the chips are down, the strong can and should ignore the restrictions of morality. There is no tribunal to call them to account for doing so, so the clear-sighted, the men of business and men of power, will not terrify themselves with the illusion that there is.

Socrates makes some conspicuously feeble moves in reply to Thrasymachus, apparently attempting to show that government is always in the interest of the governed. He emerges from the thickets with the extraordinary claim that 'no branch of expertise or form of authority procures benefit for itself' (I, 346e), a speculation already refuted by Thrasymachus's previous example of a herdsman who exercises expertise and authority over his cattle, not in their interest but in his own (I, 343b). Perhaps the dialectic at this point is deliberately ineffectual, highlighting the difficulty in meeting Thrasymachus's challenge, and the magnitude of the task in front of Socrates. Socrates only pulls himself together by introducing what now becomes the leading theme of the rest of the book: the attempt to show that morality and virtue coincide with happiness. The point of entry (again, after some irritating swordplay) is the converse association between immorality and discord. Immorality in groups makes for discord, both internally and in external dealings. But by parity, so does immorality in the single individual:

And when it (immorality) arises within a single individual, it will, I suppose, produce exactly the same results – the results it is inherently bound to have. First, it will make him incapable of action, because of internal dissension and discord; second, as well as generating internal hostility, it will generate hostility between him and moral people. Right? (I, 352a)

This gives the green light for Socrates to canter towards

the finishing line, or at any rate the end of the first book. He does so by introducing a pivotal analogy between the mind of a person and other parts with a job to do: eyes, ears and other organs. These have a function, and Socrates easily persuades Thrasymachus that 'in the absence of their goodness' eyes and ears will not perform their function properly (bad eyes mean impaired vision and bad ears impaired hearing). The mind too has functions: 'the exercise of authority, planning, and so on' as well as safeguarding 'one's way of life' (I, 353d). So, by the parallel with eyes and ears, a bad mind will handle these functions badly, and a good mind will do them well. And then, briskly, since morality is a good mental state, and immorality a bad one, the moral person will live a good life and the immoral person a bad life. But anyone living a good life is 'happy and fulfilled'. Hence, the moral person will be happy and fulfilled, and the immoral person not, and moral-ity is more rewarding than immorality.

Plato presents Thrasymachus as silenced by this display of conjuring, or perhaps his taciturn answers suggest that he is simply fed up, and he certainly seems to sulk for much of the rest of *Republic*. On the face of it, he has plenty to complain about. Let him concede that the mind's function is one of planning and safeguarding. His whole point is that this is done best by exploiting one's own strength and taking advan-tage of the weakness of others. This, of course, must be done strategically, since if one's doings will offend the law of fashion, prudence, itself one of the mind's functions for safeguarding its owner, will properly dictate caution. But in other cases, the well-functioning mind might as well be the Machiavellian mind. Let dog eat dog, and the weak go to the wall.

Socrates seems to be aiming at the conclusion that bad behaviour must result in an inner disharmony, a psychological fracture that destroys happiness or well-being, as if the Athenian envoys are bound to suffer stress or guilt or remorse for what they have done. But this is entirely unhistorical: a historically displaced Christian among the Athenian envoys might have found the episode stressful, although through the centuries the behaviour of Christian colonists, for example, suggests otherwise. But the aristocratic warrior ethic of the Athenians had not yet been contaminated, or improved, by an influx of Christian values of universal charity, forgiveness, meekness and the rest. In his history Thucydides does not report the envoys as sleeping unsoundly, although in his telling of the tale there is a suggestion that there is something *shocking*, to him as there is to us, about their unvarnished realpolitik.[5] Even if they did sleep badly, Thrasymachus can say, as Nietzsche said two thousand years later, that the bad conscience is a disease.[6] Health would mean tripping serenely back to their ships with their hearts light at a job well done.

CHAPTER 3

The Ring of Gyges

People do wrong whenever they think they can, so they act morally only if they're forced to, because they regard morality as something which isn't good for one personally. (II, 360c)

With Thrasymachus silenced or sulking, his case is taken up by Glaucon, a character identified with one of Plato's brothers, while the only significant other character, Adeimantus, is identified with a different brother. In the dialogue, they seem more or less interchangeable. Glaucon refines and adds precision to Thrasymachus's own scatter-shot attempt at saying what he means. First, he carefully separates the question of whether morality is a benefit in itself, from whether it is only useful as a means to other ends (for instance, social acceptability, the result achieved by following the law of fashion). Socrates maintains both. So Glaucon tries to show that in fact people only practise morality when they lack the ability to do wrong, and seeks to show this by a story, or thought-experiment. A shepherd from Lydia (a part of Western Asia Minor, now Turkey), Gyges, is supposed to have acquired a magic ring that rendered its wearer invisible.

Armed with it he enters the royal palace, seduces the queen, kills the king and usurps the throne. This is a highly satisfactory outcome from Gyges's point of view, so who wouldn't do the same?

> Suppose there were two such rings, then – one worn by our moral person, the other by the immoral person. There is no one, on this view, who is iron-willed enough to maintain his morality and find the strength of purpose to keep his hands off what doesn't belong to him, when he is able to take whatever he wants from the market-stalls without fear of being discovered, to enter houses and sleep with whomever he chooses, to kill and to release from prison anyone he wants, and generally to act like a god among men. (II, 360b)

In other words, separate morality from its effects, and you will see that everyone regards it as a nuisance, an annoying brake on their freedom of action.

Glaucon does not stop there, but presses the point with a further argument. Put side by side a moral person and an immoral one. Now strip the moral person of his 'aura', and give him a reputation for immorality, sufficient to subject him to all the punishments the law can inflict, and eventual death. And imagine the immoral person clever enough to enjoy all the rewards that the appearance of morality gives, but with the added benefit of being able to profit from his immorality whenever he can get away with it. Clearly the second has the richer, more successful, better rewarded life. In Greek theology it is even suggested that the gods smile on him, since being wealthier he can offer them better sacrifices (362c). Adeimantus chimes in:

> We find that not a single one of you self-styled supporters
> of morality has ever found fault with immorality or
> commended morality except in terms of the reputation,
> status, and rewards which follow from them. (II, 366e)

The challenge could not be clearer: show that morality, in and of itself and regardless of its consequences, benefits the possessor, and that immorality similarly harms him. For if this cannot be shown, the law of fashion is all that there is, and we have no answer to the Athenian envoys and their successors. The challenge echoes down the history of moral philosophy. In the eighteenth century David Hume posed the same problem in terms of the 'sensible knave' who takes advantage of the gains of cooperation and convention within society, but stands ready to cheat on them when he can gain by doing so.[1] Plato's thought-experiment merely shows us someone for whom this cheating is made especially easy.

From now on we shall call this Glaucon's challenge. It might be ducked by playing the religious theme of life after death, with heaven for the good and hell for the wicked. But the hope of evading punishment or of being given a bribe or bonus, even by a supernatural agency, and even over a long haul into eternity, is really irrelevant to Glaucon's challenge, as Adeimantus his brother insists. The whole point is that talk of rewards, either in this life or in one to come, is inadequate unless the rewards are of a kind that cannot possibly be achieved by immorality, or cannot be forfeited in spite of morality. We should act from principle, not from hope or fear, or, as Kant later put it, our moral motivation has to be *pure*, free from the calculus of self-interest.

The topic is often described by commentators as that of justice in the soul. This sounds a bit precious. But 'the soul' here is not a 'ghost in the machine'. It is simply the person considered in respect of character, knowledge and motivations. As for justice, I usually follow the modern tendency to prefer putting it in terms of the relationship between morality in general and the internal, psychological harmony or discord of the agent. I shall therefore talk of the well-ordered or rightly ordered agent. The aim is to describe this right ordering or harmony so that it satisfies two conditions. First, it must correspond to the agent doing what is right, possessing the virtues we esteem, behaving well. Second, *Republic* wants to make the benefit to the rightly ordered agent apparent without invoking other benefits such as reputation or popularity. It is to be a benefit in itself.

It is important to bear this dual aspect in mind. Glaucon would not be answered if Socrates simply described a tranquil or serene agent, for example. Tranquillity and serenity no doubt benefit their possessor. They are pleasant states to be in. But they may have little to do with virtue or behaving well – in the myth, the ring of invisibility could have enabled Gyges to commit his crimes in serenity and peace of mind. As was suggested above, the Athenian envoys may have been serene enough about what they were doing. If there is a connection, it would need arguing for.

CHAPTER 4

The Analogy

Wouldn't we say that morality can be a property of whole communities as well as of individuals? (II, 368e)

To meet Glaucon's challenge Socrates makes the move that dictates everything that follows. He suggests that morality may exist in communities as much as in individuals, and that since communities are bigger than individuals, it may be easier to see what morality truly consists in by first studying them. By investigating the well-ordered community, in which morality or justice, or the right and harmonious ordering, is found in the body politic, we can better understand it in the individual. It's a very attractive idea, but its success is bound to depend upon the kind of mapping that can be made from the body politic to the individual. For example, the question of whether a state is rightly ordered will be one about the relations between its members. So what corresponds to this in an agent? An agent, considered as a mind or soul, does not *have* members. As a person, at best I have qualities and properties. I think things, want some things, fear others, and so forth. But how do these different features correspond to the individual citizens within a community? If the correspondence is weak or fanciful, the comparison may not be much use after all.

In general it is useful to distinguish three parts of any analogy. There is the *positive* part of the analogy, the *negative* part, and the open ground in the middle, the part that may or may not make the analogy fruitful. Consider the classic scientific analogy between a gas and a container of bouncing billiard balls, which is the model at the heart of the kinetic theory of gases. The positive part of the analogy is that molecules, like billiard balls, have velocity and momentum, that their direction can change as they collide with the sides of the container that holds them, that they therefore exert force on the walls of their container, and that they can be more or less densely packed. The negative part is, for instance, that billiard balls are large enough to handle, are manufactured, cost money, and are variously coloured. None of these features is of any interest to the way the model is to be used – but neither do they constitute disanalogies that damage the point of the comparison. Open ground in the middle might be that billiard balls have a finite size, and that when they become quite densely packed they bump into each other more than if they are thinly scattered: these features are just the ones in which the analogy directs us to think about and that might prove suggestive and fruitful, as in fact they did.

We should bear this in mind when we contemplate the 'utopian' character of the republic that Plato is about to sketch. There is no doubt that he himself is often taken to be the grandfather of utopian writings in general, the ancestor of endless visionary books about Arcadia, the Golden Age, the Land of Cockaigne, the Garden of Eden, or the Islands of the Blest. There are some plums in this pudding such as Thomas More's *Utopia* of 1515, or Samuel Butler's *Erewhon* of 1872, but in general utopian writings have a bad image nowadays. They often sound weird, impractical, visionary, if not outright mad. It does not endear us, for instance, to H. G. Wells that he wrote at least five books sketching utopias, of which *A Modern Utopia* of 1905 is probably the only one remembered. We tend to respond better to books in which our fears have been realized and things have gone wrong – not books that articulate their author's dreams and ideals, but ones which reveal and focus our fears, such as George Orwell's *1984*. Hell is always easier to paint than heaven.

However, the points just made about the use of analogy help to rebut the charge of utopianism. If *Republic* is read as presenting a thought-experiment, it may not matter if there are unrealistic elements in it. They may be irrelevant to the point being made, and there is ample evidence that Plato does not care if his ideal community cannot actually exist. This does not automatically imply that he incurs the charge of irrelevant dreaming. For comparison, consider one of the most famous thought-experiments in the history of science. Faced with the Aristotelian theory that a heavy body falls much faster than a lighter body, Galileo asks us to imagine a falling weight in the form of a dumbbell (two heavy ends connected by a thin bar). Now imagine the bar becoming progressively thinner, until it is a mere wisp, and then imagine that it is finally severed completely. Is it really credible that the resulting weights suddenly slow down at this last moment, when they cease to be one and become two? With a jerk? Now, it is irrelevant to the power of this thought-experiment to protest (for instance) that nobody could fall alongside the dumbbell for long enough or with control enough to effect the final snip, so that the scenario is 'impractical'. Similarly, it may be irrelevant to the purposes for which Plato is using his thought-experiment to protest about impractical elements in the design of the community. It all depends on what the positive analogy tells us about the open ground in the middle.

So let us return to the comparison with our minds. A mind can be thought of as composite, an aggregate of features just as a city is an aggregate of people. It can be thought of as 'modular' like a Swiss army knife, in which different tools do different jobs. It can be thought of as integrated or harmonious, or by contrast fragmented and disorderly, just as a city can be. So Plato has an ample starting point, a positive part which gets the analogy off the ground. And in fact the modularity he is going to rely upon is not at all complex. He sees the soul as built from faculties, just as the city contains different classes with different kinds of job. As in the famous image of the charioteer from the *Phaedrus* (246a), the soul is thought of as tripartite. There is the charioteer, reason, attempting to control the two horses, which we can label desire and spirit. The correspondence is with three classes in society. The ruling elite likewise controls the auxiliaries or military wing, and the shoemakers and the rest who produce the goods and services on which the city relies – the artisans.

Obviously, there is an ample negative part to the analogy as well. In a state some citizens are rich and some poor. They relate to each other by trade. But nothing in the mind counts as the 'wealth' of an individual faculty or feature, nor can we well imagine one faculty, reason, say, trading with another, such as desire. But this negative analogy may not matter. It will hinge on whether the open ground in the middle proves fruitful, and that must wait on the development. Hence, we should neither embrace the analogy uncritically nor dismiss it at the outset: everything will depend on how the comparison unfolds.

Socrates believes that communities are formed when people find they are not self-sufficient, but have requirements that involve the assistance of others. For a group or community to be effective it cannot be that everyone does every job. There has to be specialization if things are to be rightly ordered. In individual arts and crafts there will be only some people who know what to do and when to do it. There will arise mechanisms of exchange, internal and external trade, and gradual expansion as people's wants expand and specialists become capable of meeting them. But with expansion comes encroachment on neighbours' land, and with that comes war, requiring yet another specialization, that of the military. With this comes the need for government, the need for the 'guardians' or the ruling elite. These have one specialist function: the management of the community. They are the custodians of the community welfare. They require a special combination of abilities. First, they will need to be courageous, passionate and strong.

> However, they should really behave with civilized gentleness towards their friends and neighbours and with ferocity towards their enemies. Otherwise it won't be a question of waiting for others to come and destroy them: they'll do the job first themselves. (II, 375c)

At first sight these are contradictory qualities, but Socrates reminds the audience that domestic farm dogs, for instance, are bred for just this combination of gentleness towards friends and flocks, and aggression towards things that threaten them. The combination also requires knowledge. The farm dog can tell its friends from strangers, and the ruling elite need to do something similar, for which they too will need education (II, 376a).

To us there is an obvious split between the military and the political. Military rule is one system, but not the best. For Plato it is not so clear. When he introduces his idea of the rulers, the famous 'guardians', he seems to blend the two, requiring a member of his elite to be both 'passionate, quick on his feet, and strong' (military virtues) and also to have 'a philosopher's love of knowledge' (a ruler's virtue; see II, 376c). It rapidly becomes clear, however, that what really matters to Plato is the function of protecting order in the state and sustaining its stability: the job of the ruling elite. Later on he does split the elite into two. There are the real ruling class, who eventually turn out to be philosophers, and purely military or policing functions belong to the next class down who are called 'auxiliaries' (II, 414b). They are told by the elite what to do. To us, this makes it a bit odd that at the beginning the real elite had to be strong and passionate as well as capable of ruling wisely. We don't expect our political class to be good shots and fast runners. They have enforcement agencies to do that for them. But Plato seems unable to bring himself entirely to separate fitness to rule from military prowess. Greece was not very far from its heroic age (Socrates's popularity seems largely to have stemmed from his awesome fortitude as a soldier).

So far Socrates may seem to have given a perfectly plausible story about the evolution of civil community. But beneath the surface there are currents which may already make readers uneasy. For example, he holds both that it is impossible that anyone should be suited for more than one task, and that the state or community has the right to prohibit anyone who tries, such as a shoemaker who tries to farm or weave or build (II, 374b). Good order, for Plato, implies a 'principle of specialization' or principle of single-mindedness. Shoemakers make shoes, and rulers rule, and this can be enforced by the collective. It also determines the kind of education different people are to get, as we shortly see. Even worse, the differential breeding and education of the ruling elite is already foreshadowed. In short an authoritarian, perhaps totalitarian, tone can already be heard. The question of how much this matters completely divides Plato's critics from his admirers.

The view that *Republic* is little more than an apology for the totalitarian state was voiced in Britain in the 1930s and 1940s, when the rise of Hitler's Germany and Stalin's Soviet Union made totalitarianism a matter of some anxiety. The charge was put fairly mildly by the left-wing Member of Parliament and classical scholar Richard Crossman, in his book *Plato Today*, published in 1937, and much more forcibly by Sir Karl Popper, in the first volume of his three-book classic of polemics, *The Open Society and its Enemies*, published in 1945.[1] Plato is there seen as the direct ancestor of Nazism, Stalinism, and any other system that subordinates the individual to the collective. He is also seen as the dangerous, utopian social engineer, providing blueprints for improvement regardless of the messy and recalcitrant nature of the human material with which he has to work.

The intemperate nature of Popper's attack in particular led to energetic rebuttals from the succeeding and contemporary generation of Plato scholars. There are two main lines of defence. The first stresses that Plato is not offering a blueprint for anything. Socrates several times says that neither the perfectly moral person, nor the imagined community which is to provide a model for him, need exist (e.g. V, 472d–e, or IX, 592b). It does not matter whether it is even possible that it should exist, or whether it is purely a thought-experiment. The second defence reminds us that the political philosophy of *Republic* is subordinate to the moral philosophy. The political descriptions are there in order to help answer Glaucon's challenge. Morality, right order or justice in the state is the magnifying glass with which we can see those things in the individual self. So features of the state that might offend us, such as its coercive power over its members, need not do so, if they drop out of the analogy when it is put to use.

The first defence can only get us so far. Let us agree that it is perfectly in order to sketch an ideal without caring whether it is or can be realized. This is not pointless fantasy. Ideals can motivate us: we can work towards them, trying to model ourselves or our community on them. We can use them as a rule or template with which to judge how far short we fall. They can inspire us. But Crossman or Popper can then put their objection in exactly those terms: look what happens when you are inspired by the totalitarian, authoritarian, collectivist ideal. You get Hitler and Stalin, either of whom might themselves have invoked *Republic* as their blueprint. Even movement towards Plato's ideal state tramples on values of democracy, egalitarianism and freedom. Far from providing an ideal, Plato has provided the road to a nightmare.

This reply is right as far as it goes, but remains far from conclusive. It all depends on what movement 'towards' an ideal is supposed to be. The vicious dictator, preying on both his own people and on neighbours, may not represent a 'step' towards the society Plato is imagining. He is not a step towards the human equivalent of the well-trained sheepdog. Neither Hitler nor Stalin has made the first step of ascent towards the character that alone qualifies someone as a ruler, and there is much more about this to come in *Republic*. Their radical, ghastly imperfections mean that nothing they could provide by way of government counts even as a move towards good order, the rule of morality in the state. That is indeed why Popper can terrify us by invoking them. It is why we fear them so much. But it also means that one cannot cite their infirmities as an objection to the ideal state of *Republic*.

This reply works, but at a cost. It is indeed true that Hitler represented no kind of candidate for Plato's ruling elite. But the authoritarian or totalitarian state clearly shares many features with the ideal republic. If, simply in virtue of those features, we find it abominable, then the whole plan of *Republic* is compromised, unless indeed these features can be regarded as dispensable.

This leads to the second defence, which reminds us that the political is only offered as a magnifying glass. When we look at right order and morality in the soul, incidental features of the political state may drop out altogether. And perhaps among those incidental features are the ones involved in democracy and liberalism, and which appear to be threatened as the Platonic state develops. To take a crude example, it may be quite impossible to see what in an individual moral agent would count as there being a voting procedure (or no voting procedure) among the members of a body politic. In that case the absence of such a procedure in Plato's state would be no obstacle to its intended use as a signpost to what would count as right order and morality in an agent.

When Plato talks of coercion in the body politic, this rings alarm bells. But if the analogy is with self-control in the individual mind, then perhaps it need not do so. Self-control in an individual may be good where control of the individual by the collective is not.

This reply is also correct as far as it goes, but it also gives rather a lot of ground – more than many Platonists would like. Used indiscriminately, the defence only works by undercutting the value of the analogy in the first place. More than that, it is hard to believe that *Republic* has nothing interesting to say about politics. And it is impossible to accept that Plato's construction is as tight as is here implied, as if everything is and remains subordinate to the business of meeting Glaucon's challenge. Plato *relishes* the details of his state, and gives far more of them than he can transport back into the analogy with the mind. For example, some of the most notorious proposals to come concern property ownership and distribution, the equality of the sexes, eugenic policies in which the rulers lie to people about whom they may marry and when they may copulate for the sake of improving the race, and even the banishment of artists from the state. But how can those be part of the positive analogy? How would we model them in the well-ordered mind? I myself may or may not be a paragon of virtue. But in so far as I am, it can't be because some part of me, such as reason, possesses no property, or educates another part, the women, in the same way as the men. It cannot be because one module or feature lies to another about the right person with whom to have a baby. These features belong to the negative part of the analogy. We cannot transport them across to gain any illumination about the individual mind, and what would make it just or well ordered. Hence, when we find Plato devoting pages to them, we must suspect that the politics has taken on a life of its own. Glaucon's challenge is, at least temporarily, shelved. We remain entitled to worry about things in the ideal republic that strike us as off-colour. One of these follows immediately.

CHAPTER 5

The Elite and the Artist

So it follows that were a man who was clever enough to be able to assume all kinds of forms and to represent everything in the world to come in person to our community and want to show off his compositions, we'd treat him as an object of reverence and awe, and as a source of pleasure, and we'd prostrate ourselves before him; but we'd tell him that not only is there no one like him in our community, it is also not permitted for anyone like him to live among us, and we'd send him elsewhere, once we had anointed his head with myrrh and given him a chaplet of wool. (III, 398a)

Plato has a simple objection to (many) poets, which is that they tell lies about the gods (as I write, the Islamic world is in uproar, synthetic or not, over some cartoons mocking the Prophet, or his legacy, so the idea is hardly unfamiliar). In Greek myths, and in Homer himself, the gods take on different shapes. They are a pretty rough bunch. Zeus, the top god, is prone to rape and to what we would call paedophilia. He constantly cheats on his wife Hera. The gods scheme and interfere with each other's plans. They are deceived and deceiving, prey to human passions like lust, anger, jealousy and envy, and are generally portrayed as carrying on much as people do. Plato is shocked by this on two counts. First, the gods are presented as less than perfect. And second, and perhaps more importantly, they are presented as *changing*.

It is here that Plato first strikes a note that becomes central later: since the divine nature is perfect it cannot be changed by external agency. But equally, it cannot change itself without changing for the worse. (Plato does not consider the possibility that God may change from one perfect state to another just as perfect. He thinks of perfect as meaning uniquely perfect, not first equal.)

> It is equally impossible, then, for God to want to change himself. Since, as we have found, the divine nature is as perfect and as good as anything could be, then any god retains his own form in a uniform, direct fashion for ever.
> (II, 381c)

This is the pregnant principle that whatever is truly good is unchanging. For the moment we simply note it, but it has incalculable consequences, including the deep and dark theory of knowledge in the central books.

Plato returns to the banishment of the artists in the last book of *Republic*, where his case is filled out by material from the central books. Here, earlier in the work, his focus remains the *mutability* of artistic representation. Not only do the gods change, but there is also the poet's ability to conjure up different characters with different thoughts, and the actor's ability to portray them in dramatic representations. Art is mobile and representations shift and change. It is wild and free. Plato's leading objection to this is the 'principle of specialization' that we have already met: the principle that regards each person as good for one thing only. A good man, then, voices good thoughts, and cannot be skilled at voicing the thoughts of a bad character.

This claim will probably strike most of us today as pretty silly. We cannot infer back from the character of Iago or Hamlet to the character of the actor playing them, nor to the character of Shakespeare who puts their words in their mouths. Even if we are mildly attached to a principle of professional specialization, in amateur dramatics we are not surprised if a shoemaker can act the part of a farmer. We might be more surprised if he could not.

But in Plato's mind something sinister remains, as if we called the theatre magical but gave the word its full disturbing weight. Perhaps rather than saying that he bases his view on the principle of specialization, we might call it a principle of purity: a monolithic view about integrity in the self, seeing pure unspotted integrity as inconsistent with even the temporary ability to act or voice anything other than its own nature. This may not be quite so alien to us as it sounds at first. There is after all something uncanny about the capacity to enter into the minds of others, so perhaps there is a grain of truth to the principle of purity, enough at any rate for us to understand comedian W. C. Fields's remark, 'show me a great actress, and you've seen the devil'. Nevertheless, the idea that drama is so bad for actors that the community ought to forego the pleasures it provides probably struck Plato's readers, just as much as it strikes us, as more than outlandish.

We can sympathize more with Plato if we transpose the idea, wondering not whether artists should be banned, but whether there is a need to ban dramatic artistry from the elite. A canker in the community that particularly frightened him was 'if the people who guard a community and its laws ignore their essence and start to pose' (421a; other translations simply have them believed to be seeming to be guardians when they are not). Here, I expect, many of us may give a shiver of recognition. We can all name posing guardians, and share Plato's view that they can destroy the community. Anything that encourages posing in public life, or leads those in public life to become skilled at posing, is a threat. We hope for purity. But, again, it is not so much acting ability that worries us as insincerity. The first is only a problem in so far as it conceals the second.

Before we mock Plato we may also reflect on our own consumption of art. The average American eighteen-year old, it is said, is likely to have watched something like 18,000 murders on TV. Although social science finds it almost impossible to speak with one voice about anything, there is good evidence that this relentless diet not only desensitizes young people, but makes them more fearful (and for that matter, more stupid). Dramatic representations give us patterns which we *can* follow, and then the question of how far children or grown-ups *do* follow them is an empirical one. Studies appear to vary, and no doubt the contagion varies with many different factors, but it is hard to believe that there is none at all.[1] Perhaps Plato is right and our minds are imitative, in which case the doings of other people and the nature of other minds are also contagious.[2] We cannot patronize Plato from a position of wisdom or success in knowing how to feed people's minds. If he were to talk not about the exile of the poets, but the exile of the entertainment executives, he would find a more sympathetic hearing.

We are much more inclined to worry whether people's minds can be harmed by too much exposure to what is bad, than to hope that they can be improved by a monocultural diet of what is good. But totalitarian states have indeed tried to control the imaginations of their subjects, by censorship and by promoting only an 'official' art in which nothing is depicted except the virtuous labours of the proletariat or the happy unity of the people in the relevant utopia. We tend to find the art dismal and the ambition fairly laughable, but living as we do in a world of mad fanaticism and routine incivility, even liberals may wonder if freedom has tipped into licence, and we have gone too far.

In other dialogues, notably *Phaedrus* and *Ion*, Plato associates artistic inspiration with divine madness: 'beautiful poems are not human, not even from human beings but are from the gods'.[3] The sentiment is at first sight flattering to the poet, and became a staple of Romanticism. It is the basis of Shelley's *A Defence of Poetry*, where the divine inspiration substitutes for reason as the measure of the ascent of the soul, and this in turn inherits centuries of Christian appropriations of Plato, equating the inspiration that is the goal of the soul's ascent with mystic union with God. But as we shall see in more detail later, it is not true to *Republic*, for which there is still ambivalence in the air. In *Ion* divine madness, possessed by the orator and reciter of verses, is expressly contrasted with knowledge which is the true result of Plato's own drama of ascent – indeed, the dialogue ends ironically, with Ion encouraged to preen himself for being inspired, and not too bothered about the fact, which Socrates has established, that he does not know anything of what he is talking about. In *Republic* the goal of the soul's ascent is unambiguously knowledge, not rapture.

We could even see Plato, at this point, as being on the side of the reality-based community. For being 'carried away' may be in some sense a divine state, but it is not the state of someone who is telling it how it is, or who is to be trusted or followed. We only have to think of the endless ills inflicted on poor humanity by orators, charismatics, seers of all kinds, in order to share Plato's mistrust. Politicians may all be bad, but visionary politicians with holy righteousness draped around them are the worst.

We may also feel rather differently about the banishment of the artists if we return to the idea that the well-ordered state is a model of the well-ordered soul. Perhaps the truly well-ordered mind would not have the capacity to enter into the doings of the fallen. In a poignant moment towards the end of *Othello* (Act IV, scene 3), Desdemona asks the more worldly Emilia if there can really be women who would cheat on their husbands, the implication being that her purity is so complete that she finds it hard to credit that there could be. If the analogy is between the presence of artistic representation in the state and the presence of vivid representations in the mind, then Desdemona is an example of Plato's ideal. She can truly say, as it were, that 'the thought never crossed my mind'. True, her purity has something inhuman about it. We might be inclined to scoff at the idea that it is ever found, human nature being what it is. But this need not bother Plato. He is talking of an ideal of purity, not the fallen human nature we see all around us. He is talking of a kind of saintliness.

The elite, then, must be brought up on a monocultural diet, only acquainted with the fine and the good. They are innocent of bad things, and that includes being innocent of representations of bad things. There is no value in any expansion of their imaginations in that direction. This may still strike us as off-key, and the reason connects with the absence of *sympathy* in Plato's conception of the virtues. We might think that however saintly Desdemona's innocence is, a gentle induction into the way of the world, such as might be provided by drama and fiction, would be an improvement. It would enable her to understand and sympathize with a wider range of human experience (it would also have enabled her to understand what was wrong with her husband in time to avoid the catastrophe). If Plato's ruling elite are brought up so that they literally cannot understand cowardice, disloyalty, greed, jealousy, and the whole range of human dispositions, then it is hard to see how they are going to be much good at ruling.

This uncovers a fundamental divide between the Classical aesthetic and the Romantic worldview. Classicism insists on a complete separation between good and evil, beauty and ugliness, light and darkness, reason and passion. The good person is on the side of the one, and has as little as possible to do with the other. In contrast, the Byronic soul, the Romantic hero, experiences everything. He is acquainted with crime, passion and darkness. Christianity is ambivalent about this. It maintains an ideal of purity. But in the myth of the Fall, Christianity insists on the double nature of man, and Romanticism follows it. The moral reason that God comes to earth in Christianity is to share in human weakness – the very reason why Plato's embodiment of the ideal, whether in political or moral terms, must keep away from it.[4] It is very hard for us to imagine how, by keeping away from it, the guardians can be anything human, let alone ideal exemplars of humanity.

Republic's preoccupation with the education of the elite continues through some rather tedious discussions of which kind of music should be allowed them, and which kind of diet. They must not concentrate exclusively on physical sports, or they become brutal. The elite should avoid hypochondria, and confine their listening to something rather like military bands. The details are of little interest, but in each case the same principle of purity is involved. The best is not to be contaminated by the worst. Proportion, orderliness and lawfulness must permeate all their experience (424e). This does not, however, mean that the state must legislate for every nuance of behaviour. Order flows naturally from the right, pure, uncontaminated education. One of the attractive things about *Republic* is that Plato insists on the supremacy of education over law. If a society finds it has to issue anti-social behaviour orders to whole sections of its young people – the British government's current strategy for improving them – it has already lost.

CHAPTER 6

Glaucon's Challenge

*Isn't it the case… that when each of these three classes – the one
that works for a living, the auxiliaries, and the guardians –
performs its proper function and does its own job in the
community, then this is morality and makes the community
a moral one?* (IV, 434c)

The ruling elite are the trustees of the community's happiness.
Plato has an entirely realistic sense of the causes of dissent
and fragmentation within communities, which are centrally
located in disparities of wealth and sexual success. Hence the
Spartan communism of the guardians' lives. The principle of
specialization means that nothing must distract from their
single-minded dedication to the good of the society, and since
nothing is more distracting than concern for possessions and
for sex, these must be stripped away. So the guardians are
not allowed any possessions, and couplings are managed perfectly clinically, without room for private passion and private
possessiveness. Again, there is a precise parallel with the later
Christian ideal of sainthood, except that Plato realistically
accepts that celibacy is not for everyone, even among the elite.

Once the ruling elite is educated properly, various good things accrue to the collective, at any rate so long as they are ruling. They embody genuine wisdom. They can also guarantee courage, for in Plato courage is an exercise of wisdom: 'the retention of the notion, which has been inculcated by law through the agency of education, about what things and what kinds of things are to be feared' (IV, 429c). Their rule is equivalent to self-discipline, the control of the lower by the higher, which is also the mastery of pleasure and desire. Finally, the morality of the state consists in this order and discipline, the embodiment of the principle that everyone should keep their place, the principle of specialization.

This last claim and the way it is unveiled particularly irritated Sir Karl Popper. Plato only reveals it after a fair amount of tedious dramatic build-up by Socrates, in which he presents himself as a hunter, first daunted by the fugitive quarry, then getting a glimpse of it, finally leaping on the principle in triumph (IV, 432c–434c). Popper sees fiendish literary cunning in this, a plot whereby the reader is lulled into thinking that Socrates is being carefully watched by Glaucon, so that the reader need not be on guard at all: 'I cannot interpret it as anything but an attempt – it proved to be highly successful – to lull the reader's critical faculties, and, by means of a dramatic display of verbal fireworks, to divert his attention from the intellectual poverty of this masterly piece of dialogue.'[1] There may be something to Popper's suspicion, but it is equally possible that Plato has other reasons for presenting the philosopher as a kind of hunter. He is well aware that other people are apt to regard the philosopher as a kind of wimp (V, 549e–550b), so the contrary implication of courage and skill in the philosophical quest is unlikely to be accidental.[2]

It is true that there is much to dislike in the idea that the principle of specialization is the key to morality, either in a collective or in an individual. In its political application it seems, as it did to Popper, little more than a principle for denying the bulk of the population any say in how they are governed. Evidently, for Plato, there is nothing particularly valuable in people having a say in their own affairs, or in being able to register dissent even from those who know better than they do. It is important, of course, that the ruling elite *does* know better than the shoemakers and the rest (although there is a serious problem about how the rabble are supposed to recognize this). But even so, we value individuality. The tyranny of those who know is still a tyranny. Parents with teenagers may genuinely know better what is in their children's best interest. But it does not follow and is not true that the best regulated family is one in which the teenager has no choice over how to live and no space to experiment. Making our own mistakes has a value of its own. It is a corollary of the value we place on freedom and individuality, closely connected, obviously, to the value we have already stressed of thinking for oneself, embodied by the liberal Socrates of other dialogues.

Here, then, is a point at which defence of *Republic* best

takes the tack of insisting that the political is only an analogy with the individual moral self. This is textually justified, for Socrates immediately turns to the individual to see how the match goes:

> What we have to do now is apply the results we found in the case of the community to an individual. If there is a match, that will be fine; but if we find something different in the case of an individual, then we'll return to the community to test the new result. With luck, the friction of comparing the two cases will enable morality to flare up from these fire-sticks, so to speak, and once it's become visible we'll make it more of a force in our own lives.
> (IV, 434e–435a).

So how does the idea stand up when we confine it to the individual?

The analogy is supposed to work because the ruling elite is parallel to reason, the auxiliaries or military is parallel to the 'spirited' part of the self, and the artisans are parallel to particular appetites and passions, of which Plato's favourite examples are lust, hunger and thirst. The principle on which the self is divided into these 'parts' is not obvious, and Plato takes his time over it. The central fact from which he starts is the possibility of conflict within the individual: the conflict, for instance, between calm self-interest and raging appetite, or disgust and curiosity (IV, 439e). Once there is the possibility of conflict, it is to be approached by thinking of parties to the conflict 'as if they were different things' (IV, 440a). And this does indeed seem inevitable. Conflict is bound to be represented in terms of hypothesized traits: shame versus desire, temperance versus greed, prudence versus pleasure. It is the same train of thought that was later magnified by Freud, when he takes the simultaneous presence of contradictory impulses in a person to suggest the existence of a whole unconscious mind, a set of desires and beliefs with their own coherence whose occupants are hidden from the subject. Plato does not need this extravagance, but only the presence of individual desires and tendencies, bundled together under the tripartite heading of reason, 'spirit' and desire.[3]

CHAPTER 7

The Man of Spirit

Why the trio? On the face of it we might make do with reason and desire. Most modern attempts to represent behaviour do so, supposing that desire or preference determine what we aim at, while reason determines our awareness of what is around us and therefore our capacity to fulfil our desires. In this picture 'reason' is far from sovereign. As David Hume famously put it:

> We speak not strictly and philosophically when we talk of the combat of passion and of reason. Reason is, and ought only to be the slave of the passions, and can never pretend to any other office than to serve and obey them.[1]

On this scheme what we incorrectly call a battle between reason and passion is in fact a battle between two rather different passions, such as a calm desire for good reputation against a hot desire for revenge or a spasm of lust. Nor can desires themselves properly be criticized as 'unreasonable', except in the sense either that they depend upon mistaken beliefs, or coincide with mistaken beliefs about what is needed for their fulfilment. In either case it is, properly speaking, the beliefs that are unreasonable.

This scheme leaves plenty of room, however, for desires or passions to attract criticism on other grounds. They may be imprudent, or excessive, or misdirected, immature, hurtful, unimaginative, and best suppressed on all sorts of grounds. They may be actively malevolent, or bitter or twisted. According to Stoics and Buddhists, it would be better to have as few as possible. What desires and passions cannot be is true or false, and it is the province of reason to distinguish truth and falsity.

Hume's scheme is not compulsory – indeed, it marks one of the most contested areas of contemporary moral theory. It certainly seems to mark a distinct rupture with Plato (and Aristotle), and Hume may have intended it to do so. But Plato's own scheme is itself far from clear. For example, it is not very clear to what extent reason in Plato is itself partly a creature of passion – a kind of erotic passion belonging to those who have fallen in love with wisdom or to those who obtain adequate ideas of things. Down the centuries, the picture has often been complicated by the association between passions and 'the body', contrasted with more rarefied intellectual emotions lying in the mind, notably the intellectual love of God. That in turn is a phenomenon that simply must not admit of any partition into the intellectual bit and the love bit, since that would open the horrifying possibility of, on the one hand, understanding God and regarding him with amusement or contempt, or, on the other hand, properly loving God without grasping his nature at all. All in all, it is unwise to attempt any description of how Western thought has tried to relate reason and passion.

In any case Plato has quite other fish to fry when he advanced his tripartite scheme. His distinction between 'spirit' and appetite or desire, for instance, works largely to signal different pathologies of the soul, or different ways in which people can fail to be well ordered.[2]

'Spirit', or *thumos* as Plato calls it, corresponds to those trusty assistants of the shepherd, the sheepdogs. They are the armed wing of government, there to give effect to the determinations of the elite. At least some of the time, Plato seems to have in mind a special kind of desire or passion, associated with pride or shame or *amour-propre* or honour – the kind of 'spirit' that just will not allow you to let yourself go, make a pig of yourself, succumb to this or that prick of desire. This is how it is described at *Phaedrus*, 253e, where the equation between the spirited horse and shame is explicit. It is also the way conflict arises within the poor creature Leontius, who had a quasi-sexual curiosity to gaze at recently executed corpses, and who was angry or disgusted with himself as a result of either possessing or indulging this shameful desire (IV, 439e). For Hume the question arises whether Leontius's shame is not properly just another desire, the desire to conform to Locke's law of fashion for example, or in other words to stand well in the eyes of others. Or, if it is not simply that, it may be a concern that has developed from that, such as Adam Smith's 'man within the breast' who represents the voices of other people without. Or, it may be fear engendered by parental pressures in infancy. In that case a better architecture might be initially a simple dualism of reason and desire, and secondarily a division of desire into those that are connected with honour, including our sense of shame, and the others: appetites which may be good or bad, but whose strength and direction is in principle capable of being shameless, wayward and wanton.

In fact *thumos* is not simply a sense of shame. Its emblem is the lion to which it is explicitly compared in Book IX (588d), as much as the sheepdog. It has more to do with the psychology of the warrior-aristocrat, the jealousy of honour, and the desire for glory. The paradigm of the spirited man, in classical times, was the Achilles of Homer's *Iliad*, the ultimate action-man, the embodiment of touchy honour and military heroism. At the opening of the book, Achilles's honour is slighted by Agamemnon, the commander-in-chief of the Greek forces. Achilles feels shamed in front of the army, so he withdraws and sulks, becoming useless to the Greek army. It is only when his bosom companion, Patroclus, gets himself killed by Hector that Achilles rouses himself. Achilles knows that if he slays Hector he will himself die shortly afterwards, and he regards death as dreadful – he is in love with life. But he chooses death and glory, running amok on the battlefield, killing Hector and desecrating his body, and en route committing the atrocity of sacrificing twelve Trojan prisoners on Patroclus's funeral pyre. Achilles eventually gives up Hector's body only when touched by the tears of Hector's father, King Priam.

Achilles is a problem, as are lions. He is petulant, and his raw ferocity is about as likely to be directed against Agamemnon as against the enemy, and very nearly is so, while in the grip of his anger he commits unpardonable atrocities. He is intemperate and immoderate, doing everything to excess. Nevertheless he has glamour, that of the man of mettle or the hero. He is a permanent magnet to weaker spirits: Alexander the Great self-consciously adopted him as a role model, and Aryan 'manliness' was a preoccupation of Nazi ideology. No democratic politician dares to slight this glamour. Today one need only think of George W. Bush posturing on an aircraft carrier, or the people of California electing a cardboard action-man as their governor, or the universal tendency among British politicians to feign an interest in football. As an aside I should say that it is, however, a small mark of progress that while as late as 1964 the art critic Sir Kenneth Clark could talk of his Victorian predecessor John Ruskin as having an intellectual's 'girlish passion for soldiers', the reference to girls now grates on us, and the allure is surely more likely today to enchant immature members of the male sex.[3]

In any case, Clark, and perhaps Ruskin, completely misunderstood Plato on the matter, imagining that he himself was captivated by the military regime of Sparta and using it as a model for his ideal republic. On the contrary, for Plato, someone like Achilles would be far from ideal, and his *thumos* is a problem. Plato wants his ferocity and his desire for glory to be curbed by calmer forces. It does not much matter whether we call these other forces 'reason' or long-term or civilized 'desires'. They must include such things as loyalty, or concern for civil order, or proportion. Even Achilles's estimate of death is wrong, for, as we later learn, the wise man will be unmoved by its terrors.

In *The Art of Rhetoric* Aristotle later captured the psychological profile of men of *thumos* that Plato is bothered about:

> passionate, keen-tempered, carried away by anger and unable to control their *thumos*. For owing to their love of honour they cannot bear to be slighted, but become indignant if they think they are being wronged. However, though they love honour they love victory even more: for youth longs for superiority and victory is a kind of superiority… And they are more courageous, for they are full of *thumos* and hope, and the former quality prevents them from feeling fear while the latter gives them confidence… and they would rather perform noble actions than useful ones: for they live according to their habitual character rather than calculation, and calculation aims at the useful, while virtue aims at the noble… they do everything to excess; they love to excess, and they hate to excess, and everything else in the same way… They do wrong as a result of arrogance and overreaching rather than wickedness.[4]

Plato knows the allure of this character. Indeed, it will be part of his worry about the deleterious effect of drama and poetry that it is exactly this kind of character that makes for pleasurable drama. There are more stories about action-men than about philosophers, and they seduce more young people than sages ever do.

So Plato is far from celebrating the ideal of 'manliness'. In fact, it is one of Friedrich Nietzsche's gripes about him that his philosophy has a pale and sickly aspect, actively opposing the 'will to power', the struggle for ascendancy, the will of life itself.[5] But Nietzsche simplified, since Plato does not oppose the presence of *thumos* in the soul. He wants it, but he wants it properly tamed. In particular he wants us to reconfigure our conception of courage, separating it from the raw will to power, the martial spirit and the desire for military glory. Courage is not an arrogant disposition to run amok, but something more like the steadfastness or fortitude that Socrates exhibits, a trait demanding above all the clear-sighted understanding of a situation and what it demands. Perhaps the most prominent signal of this is the celebrated gender equality of *Republic*. Women as well as men are capable of joining the ruling elite. Translated back into the well-ordered soul, this means that female virtue is identical with male virtue, and this itself drives a cleft between virtue and 'manliness'.

CHAPTER 8

Specialization

> *There's nothing more disastrous for the community, then, than*
> *the intrusion of any of the three classes into either of the other*
> *two, and the interchange of roles among them, and there could*
> *be no more correct context for using the term 'criminal'.*
>
> (IV, 434b)

In Plato's state the principle of specialization is the heart of morality. The well-ordered state requires that rulers rule, the auxiliaries do their military and policing duties, while the productive classes get on with their allotted jobs. It is a caste system, and the castes are ossified. Plato expresses nothing but a caustic aristocratic disdain for anyone who tries to get out of their own caste. He would allow no Working Men's education, no Open University, no lifelong opportunities for bettering oneself. Those condemned to 'tawdry commercial activities' are under a life sentence. There is no parole. Like later aristocrats down through history, if there is one thing Plato cannot stand it is a nouveau riche, a parvenu.

We do not like caste systems, and hence rebel against this in the name of several values: individualism, humanitarianism, liberty, equality. So this is one of those places where Platonists do best to shelter behind the point of the analogy, which is to use the state to cast light on the nature of the well-ordered individual. Perhaps what strikes us as illiberal, and vilely so, about the proposed state is part of the negative analogy, but becomes harmless or even illuminating when we think of the well-ordered soul. Thought of politically, Plato is advocating the subservience of the individual to the collective, the very essence of totalitarianism. But thought of individually, he may only be advocating that the psychological harmony of the individual is a value that must suppress a lop-sided development of one part at the expense of others: too much spirit, or unbridled appetites, for example. There is no room here for a charge of totalitarianism, since it is surely harmless to urge that it is well-being of the whole totality, the whole agent considered in all his or her mental aspects, that is the aim. Of course, if this is the way it works, then any results are achieved in spite of the comparison between the state and the soul rather than because of it. The state is not so much a magnification of the soul as an imperfect and unreliable guide to what we might hope for it.

But does the analogy work in any event? There are certainly points of weakness. For a start, while it is easy to imagine a badly-ordered self, it is impossible to imagine one in which desires do not do their own job. We can imagine someone qualified for shoemaking chucking it in and becoming a not-so-good soldier. But we cannot make sense of thirst 'taking over' the job of shame, or lust taking over the function of a desire to learn more about astronomy. Thirst is thirst, and lust is lust. Disorder in the state arises when individual people try to crawl out of the role to which they are fitted. But desires are defined by their objects, and cannot themselves take on different roles again (although they may be repressed, and substituted by other desires, of course).

When Plato explains what he means, it is not desires changing objects, but desires trying 'to dominate and rule over things' that bothers him (IV, 442b). So it looks as though morality in the individual is close to being equated with self-control or self-mastery, and this is a central part of Plato's thinking. Perhaps all the elaborate analogy gives us is that he is for temperance, and against wantonness and excess. Fair enough, we might say, but did we have to go through such a palaver just to get here?

In any event, it seems strange to equate self-control with the whole of morality. After all, there are cool and collected villains. In Thucydides, the Athenian envoys seemed perfectly self-controlled. They did not froth or bite the carpet or gnash their teeth, and may not even have raised their voices. They did not have to. They had what they regarded as a perfectly satisfactory ordering of passion by reason, here operating as cool, calculated understanding of where Athenian interest lay. Thrasymachus, it seems, can nod through everything that has gone on so far. He need not present himself as a champion of excess, nor of military *thumos*, nor of disorderly appetite.

The worry here concerns what is included under the

umbrella of reason. If the analogy with the ruling political elite is to hold, reason should have at least one desire of its own: concern for the well-being of the composite, which in this case means the whole individual. But that raises the question why just that concern and none other should be uniquely reasonable. In many people's minds ethics is largely a matter of getting some altruism or genuine concern for others in amongst the dominant forces of egoism or selfish concern for one's own well-being. Indeed, that is how the whole subject has been structured in many texts, including the magisterial *Method of Ethics* by the nineteenth-century Cambridge philosopher Henry Sidgwick.[1] It would seem high-handed, to say the least, to set things up so that concern for the well-being of others is simply invisible, or perhaps downgraded to a mere appetite, due to be governed by rampant self-interest, from the very beginning. But if reason's interest is confined to the well-being of the self, this is how it will be. We get the horrendous result that genuine altruism is not even desirable, but represents a fracture in the soul, a moment in which a passion, such as sympathy for another, escapes the proper government of reason. It is just this that must not happen in the well-ordered soul.

This worry cannot be laid to rest by taking all desires and concerns out of the domain of reason. Reason needs some concerns of its own. For, if it is cleansed of desire altogether, then it is left with no agenda, and what qualifies it to govern desires, pulling them in any particular direction, or restraining or encouraging them to any particular degree? So conceived, reason becomes no more than Hume said it was, the pure slave of the passions, able to advance truths that may guide us in pursuing what we want, but quite unable to mount forces of its own against any particular passion we happen to have.

Perhaps, then, it would be better to move in the other direction, allowing reason to have in its domain not only egoism, but some concern for the well-being of others. The Athenian envoys are not now paradigms of reason in action. Since they are immune to concern for the Melians, they must have amputated part of their reasoning selves, and therefore fail to be well ordered and just.

This can be said, certainly, but the question is whether *Republic* has earned the right to say it, and the suspicion must be that it has not. For we still have no inkling why having a well-ordered soul is going to lead to anything like a common point of view with others, the kind of tendency to take the other person's needs or requirements into consideration that the Athenian envoys so obviously lacked when it came to the Melians. We do not know why, if they pursue their purely selfish course, this will undermine their own happiness or flourishing. We do not know why the envoys, if they are to be 'reasonable', must forgo or betray Athens's apparent best interest. To put it another way, Plato may at first sight be on course to meeting Glaucon's challenge, by pulling tight a connection between a well-ordered soul and a happy one. But the well-ordering of the soul is simply a structure designed for the soul's own harmony, and can potentially coincide with letting others go hang. And so long as that is so, Thrasymachus, the Athenian envoys, and for that matter neo-conservatives and other exponents of realpolitik, have not been silenced, or even met on proper ground.

Even staunch Platonists have thrown up their hands here. Thus the great Victorian scholar George Grote thought that Plato was trying to square the circle, deriving the virtue of justice, which is in fact centrally a virtue that regards others and their interests in a balance with one's own, from the basically self-regarding or prudential aim of safeguarding the harmony of one's own soul. It would be like proving that someone who is concerned about his own health is therefore concerned, or would be concerned if he was rational, about everybody else's. It simply can't be done.[2]

CHAPTER 9

Knowledge and Belief

> *'Unless communities have philosophers as kings,' I said, 'or*
> *the people who are currently called kings and rulers practise*
> *philosophy with enough integrity – in other words, unless*
> *political power and philosophy coincide... there can be no end*
> *to political troubles, my dear Glaucon, or even to human*
> *troubles in general...' (V, 473d)*

Plato advances the claim that in the well-ordered state the ruling elite needs to be composed of philosophers, knowing in advance that it is going to make jaws drop. Before seeing why, it may be worth pointing to moderately bland things that might be meant by it. It is, after all, not so very radical to suggest that people who know relevant things make better leaders than those who do not. A guide who knows the terrain is better than a guide who has never set foot on it. A captain who knows how to sail is better than one who does not. It requires only some analogy between the job of the rulers and other craft skills to suggest that things go better if the ruling elite know their way about.

Of course, 'knowing their way about', in the case of ruling

a state, may imply a whole range of knowledge and abilities: being able to understand the motivations of people, being able to anticipate the upshot of different decisions, being imaginative enough to generate strategies for getting over a whole variety of problems, and so on. We naturally think in terms of a conglomeration of different experts: economists, strategists, planners, people sensitive to the reactions of other cultures, and so on. It is not at all radical to hold that governments need to be informed in order to work at all well. This much is still Plato-lite, although it formed a large part of the ideology of the modern world. The education of the public servants who make up the Establishment was a Victorian preoccupation, and in Britain at least it went on self-consciously in the shadow of *Republic*.[1]

The experts still have to submit their judgements to those who make the final decisions. A ruler may be told that he can afford to go to war, that he has the manpower, that the technical problems are not insuperable, but he or she still has to judge whether it is the thing to do. Here, as Plato well understood, the analogy between ruling and craft skill begins to look shaky. The mountain guide or the captain of a ship, like the shoemaker or other producer, works with reasonably fixed ends: to find the route, to complete the voyage safely and swiftly, and so on. But in judging that something is the thing to do, the ends may not be fixed. Precisely the problem may be that if you look for one outcome, then there is one way to go about it, but if you look for a different one, then there is a different thing to do – and the problem is to know which to go for. If you want acquisitions, then the thing to do might be to go to war. If you value more highly the safety of your people, it may not be. The ruler has to decide which. He has to order a plurality of possible goods.

On Hume's picture of reason and passion, that we met above, there is a point here where reason goes silent. Its function as the slave of the passions is to present the situation in all its complexity. It can present what philosophers call conditionals: *if* you want this outcome, *that* is the way to go about it, or *this* is the risk you are running. But it cannot tell you to want the outcome, or how urgent it is to avoid the risk. About that it goes silent while the passions fight for possession of the soul of the ruler, or in other words, jostle for ascendancy over the decision. What you do will depend upon what you want, and although wants can certainly be criticized in the light of other wants, eventually the whole web of desire exists with whatever shape it may have independently of reason. For Plato this is not true. There is an answer which either ranks the alternatives outright, or at worst tells you that a number tie for first place, in which case it does not matter which you choose. But when there is an answer a sufficient exercise of wisdom or understanding will enable the ruler both to find it and to control his passions so that it becomes the most attractive option for him, the thing to do. For Hume we can *say* that a ruler made a wise decision, or showed that he knew what to do, but we can't really *mean* it as Plato intends. It would be a compliment, paid because we happen to share the ruler's priorities or profile of desires and fears. It would not signal that the ruler has brought his decision into conformity with truth or reason, precisely because truth and reason are silent about overall ends.

Plato does not think like this. The charioteer controls the horses of passion and spirit; the ruler controls the martial arm and the people of the state. So the ruler first has to know what it is best to do. But this in turn raises the question of how the ruler is to gain and exercise this wisdom and understanding. So this becomes the topic, and Plato rapidly makes it clear that he has something much more radical than a well-educated civil service in mind. It is here that we get to the 'perennial philosophy' and Plato-lite turns into Plato very heavy indeed.

The crucial argument comes from V, 474d, to the end of Book V, at 480a. In outline, Socrates first gets agreement that the philosopher desires the whole of knowledge, not just some part of it (as it were, knowledge of this or that particular subject matter). In addition, and crucially, the philosopher is not just an idle sightseer or theatre-goer, content to collect diverse sights and sounds. The philosopher understands what he sees. He can get beneath the surface. He can discriminate and distinguish what is common or essential, and especially what is common or essential to the plurality of particular good or beautiful things. Mere theatre-goers and sightseers skate on the surface. They are constitutionally unable to get beyond the particulars themselves, to appreciate their common essence.

The argument now sets out to prove that the theatre-goers and sightseers live in a dream world, and by contrast the philosopher, who has the ability to see beauty and goodness themselves, lives in the real world. An equivalent way of putting it, Plato thinks, is that the philosopher has knowledge, whereas the others have only beliefs. Of course it is a little hard to convince the believers of this, and of their relatively poor state of health compared to the person of knowledge. That's just how it is: it is always difficult to persuade those who live in the dark that they are missing something. But we must accept that knowledge and belief are different faculties or capacities, for knowledge is infallible, and belief is not. And different faculties have different domains, or spheres of operation. The proper domain of knowledge is reality, while the proper domain of belief must be something different, something not quite real, since that is reserved for knowledge. It is something half real, an inferior subject. It is not entirely unreal, since that is the domain of incomprehension. Belief must find an intermediate subject-matter.

If we return to theatre-goers and sightseers, we find what this inferior subject matter is. We can ask them:

> is there is one beautiful thing, in this welter of beautiful
> things, which won't turn out to be ugly? Is there one moral
> deed which won't turn out to be immoral? Is there one just
> act which won't turn out to be unjust? (V, 479a)

The answer (surprisingly) turns out to be that there is not. Any member of a plurality 'no more *is* whatever it is said to be than it *is not* whatever it is said to be'. So now we have located the domain of belief. It is the 'welter of things' that the masses conventionally regard as one thing or another – beautiful, for example. The beauty of these things, as it were, hovers between reality and unreality, since in truth they are no more beautiful than non-beautiful, or no more good than not good. It is only the philosopher who can see beauty or goodness itself 'in its permanent and unvarying nature' who can aspire to knowledge, and hence be in touch with the real.

Even Plato's admirers (beginning with Aristotle) tend to jib at all this, and one can understand why. There is an immediate (but, we see later, superficial) objection to the whole separation of belief and knowledge as distinct faculties, therefore with distinct subject-matters. We more naturally suppose that you can know something which you previously only believed, as when you come to learn what was hitherto only conjectural, for instance by going and looking. Knowledge is true belief that has a decent pedigree, according to an account heralded in one of Plato's other dialogues, *Theaetetus*. In that case, by putting himself in a better position, one person may know what another merely believes. Someone may fear, or suspect, or even believe that there is a bear in his rubbish bin, and when he opens the lid he rapidly comes to know that there is. But what he knows is exactly what he previously suspected. There is no distinction of the domains of knowledge and belief. So here in *Republic* we seem to be offered little more than a flimsy excuse to take us away from the ordinary world, substituting instead some strange otherworldly 'permanent and unvarying' subject-matter for the philosopher.

And even if we can make sense of that, in the game with the likes of Thrasymachus and Glaucon, the move looks set to be a spectacular own-goal. If the philosopher only knows about otherworldly things, he is not likely to be at all adapted to knowing about the day-to-day problems and hand-to-mouth solutions that make up the art of government.

To some, Plato's apparent flight from the world around us has all seemed outrageous enough to make us conclude that there must be some kind of unconscious moral and emotional agenda driving him. Nietzsche diagnoses it as the sadism of the ascetic, the desire to disown and vilify everyday life, to promote a self-denying retreat from the world, a disparagement of our passions and senses and life itself. He was in no doubt about its malign influence and importance. It marks not only the beginning of the end for the golden world of classical Greece (ruled by *thumos*) but it is the side of philosophy that, vulgarized and mingled with other currents, made up the religious instinct of Christianity. It did, however, give us what Nietzsche calls the ascetic 'will to truth', which is in a sense the engine-room of Western civilization:

> Let us not be ungrateful to it, although it must certainly be conceded that the worst, most durable, and most dangerous of all errors so far was a dogmatist's error – namely, Plato's invention of pure spirit and the good as such. But now that it is overcome, now that Europe is breathing freely again after this nightmare and at least can enjoy a healthier – sleep, we, *whose task is wakefulness itself*, are the heirs of all

that strength which has been fostered by the fight against
this error. To be sure, it meant standing truth on her head
and denying *perspective*, the basic condition of all life, when
one spoke of spirit and the good as Plato did. Indeed as a
physician one might ask: 'How could the most beautiful
growth of antiquity, Plato, contract such a disease? Did the
wicked Socrates corrupt him after all? Could Socrates have
been the corrupter of youth after all? And did he deserve
his hemlock?'

But the fight against Plato or, to speak more clearly and
for 'the people', the fight against the Christian-ecclesiastical
pressure of millennia – for Christianity is Platonism for 'the
people' – has created in Europe a magnificent tension of the
spirit the like of which had never yet existed on earth: with
so tense a bow we can now shoot for the most distant goals.[2]

Immanuel Kant, himself often found guilty of the otherworldly philosophy of German idealism, put it more sympa-
thetically, and more beautifully:

The light dove, cleaving the air in her free flight, and feeling
its resistance, might imagine that its flight would be still
easier in empty space. It was thus that Plato left the world of
the senses…[3]

For Nietzsche, Plato is here the sick, sadistic ascetic who
plunged Europe into the darkness of his extra-terrestial night-
mares. For Kant, he has made a slightly more pardonable

blunder, believing that in the name of real understanding he can simply jettison the connection with sense experience which alone makes understanding possible. If this is our first encounter with a Plato that is not Plato-lite, it is not very promising.

CHAPTER 10

The Myth of the Cave

So the sun is not to be identified with sight, but is responsible for sight and is itself within the visible realm… As goodness stands in the intelligible realm to intelligence and the things we know, so in the visible realm the sun stands to sight and the things we see. (VI, 508b–c)

Plato leaves the world of the senses with the doctrine that there is a permanent and unvarying reality, a divine and orderly world 'where wronging and being wronged don't exist, where all is orderly and rational' (VI, 500c). This is obviously distinct from the shifting scenes of 'plurality and variety' (VI, 484b) which the senses show us, and in which normal life is lived. He holds the view that this reality is alone the subject of knowledge, and he is in no doubt that such knowledge is possible, although it is demanding, and only ever achieved by the elite few, the philosophers or lovers of knowledge who have undergone an arduous education before becoming capable of it. Finally, there is the view that this reality provides a foundation for ethics and right conduct. It somehow certifies, all by itself, what is virtue and what is not.

Within that framework, variation is possible. The key issue will be how to think of the relation between the 'transcendental' reality, and the world of the senses, which is after all the world in which the elite have to act, and which they are apparently qualified to rule. Plato is well aware of the problem: immediately after the passages we have been looking at, he confronts the objection that philosophers, or at least people who do not drop it after an initial dabbling education, 'turn out to be pretty weird (not to say, rotten to the core)' (VI, 487d). Socrates urges that philosophers are bound to be disrespected by the vulgar, precisely *because* they are vulgar, and therefore incapable of appreciating the true expertise that the philosopher brings to the civic community. But worse than that, in an imperfect state, the insidious corruptions of flattery and mass adulation will deflect any human being from the course of philosophy into the hurly-burly of unilluminated argument and politics. Finally, upstarts and pretenders will gatecrash philosophy, pretending themselves to possess the knowledge of the philosopher, and to the majority of people they are indistinguishable from the real thing.

All these are obstacles, serious if not entirely insuperable, to establishing the rule of the elite, the philosopher-kings. They boil down to a chicken-and-egg problem. The philosopher can only grow in the ideal community, but no community can be ideal unless already under the rule of the philosopher. To break the log-jam, it would take a 'trembling hand', a random generation of one of the necessary ingredients, after which, perhaps, both individual and community could lever themselves up the path to perfection. But by itself none of this gives us a model for the kind of Enlightenment which is needed for the philosopher-ruler.

What we need at this point is a more concrete illustration of what the elite knows, and how they bring that knowledge to bear on the everyday realities of decisions and choices. Instead, Plato gives us three images, those of the sun, the line, and the cave. The sun, in this metaphor, illuminates and lights up the visible world. Plato also suggests that it changes the things we see. At least, in the application of the metaphor:

> Well, here's how you can think about the mind as well.
> When its object is something which is lit up by truth and
> reality, then it has – and obviously has – intelligent
> awareness and knowledge. However, when its object is
> permeated with darkness (that is, when its object is
> something which is subject to generation and decay), then
> it has beliefs and is less effective, because its beliefs chop
> and change, and under these circumstances it comes
> across as devoid of intelligence. (VI, 508d)

Again we have the identification of reality, the proper object of knowledge, with the unchanging. The metaphor of the sun does not really help much with this: after all, in sunlight we see things that change just as we do in artificial light or poor natural light. Sunlight does not freeze things. All the metaphor really gives us is a vague idea of a permanent 'illumination'. Continuing, however, Plato compares the light cast by the sun with the knowledge and truth illuminated, or brought into view, or even created, by goodness itself. For goodness confers 'reality and being' on the things we know (VI, 509b).

This is hardly convincing, so to supplement the simile of the sun Plato gives us the next image, which is that of the divided line. We are to imagine a line divided into two unequal sections, with each section divided in the same ratio to two further sub-sections. In the first section of the line there is knowledge of a 'visible realm' consisting of likenesses, shadows, reflections, and so on. Then in the second section are the things whose likenesses are found in the first section: 'all the flora and fauna there are in the world, and every kind of artefact too' (VI, 510a). These together form the realm of belief, and the two sections of shadows and everyday objects stand to each other as this realm stands to the realm of knowledge – in other words, belief is to knowledge as shadow is to original. But the realm of knowledge is itself divided. Next up then is the world of the 'likenesses' which geometers use: particular diagrams, for example. Although they use these things, the object of their study is to transcend them and obtain a purely abstract understanding of geometrical forms. A diagram (which may be blurry or ill-drawn or made up of thick lines and skew triangles, and so forth) is an aid to the abstract thought, but not itself the subject-matter. Pythagoras could have worked out his famous theorem staring at a pretty terrible drawing of a right-angle triangle. But what he then contemplated was the second and highest division of the realm of knowledge (and so the fourth segment of the line). Plato associates it with the transcending of sense experience, and the arrival at a point at which nothing need be taken for granted. It is 'what reason grasps by itself, thanks to its ability to practise dialectic' (VI, 511b).

It can't be said that the metaphor of the line helps very much. There is much to dislike in the whole set-up. In the initial two sections of the line, there is the implication that the ordinary objects of sense experience are merely shadows or pictures or 'likenesses' even of everyday things, rather than those things themselves. But why should we accept that? When I see a book, I typically see neither the shadow of the book, nor a picture of the book. Plato is probably skipping down the permanent wrong turning in philosophy, which is to suppose that in order to cope with the phenomena of illusion and hallucination, we must analyse everyday straightforward perception into a 'direct' acquaintance only with a proxy for such things as books: a 'sense-datum', or some kind of see-through, mental picture of a book. The mind on this model becomes the spectator of a scene generated within itself, inside its own inner theatre, somewhere at the end of the optical and other processes whereby neurons and synapses deliver their 'messages' to it. This model of the mind and its perceptual objects is generally regarded as tempting but untenable – one sign of its untenability being that it is a royal road to scepticism, or the consequence that we are forever trapped within the selfsame inner theatre, with no access to objects outside. This is not the place to detail all the ways in which modern philosophy has sought to dismantle the idea. It is enough to signpost it as a dead end.[1]

Many philosophers have fallen for the picture of the mind as an inner theatre, and therefore acquainted with mere shadows, illusions or images – proxies standing in for external things. But usually they put up with two levels of reality: that of ideas or images (the shadows) and that of real external things themselves. Plato is much more complex, using the line to model a four-fold division of reality. The next layer is indeed that of 'ordinary' things, things that are changing, including such everyday things as flora, fauna and artefacts. However, these cannot themselves be objects of knowledge, but not because we fall victim to scepticism whenever we try to get one step beyond the images in the inner theatre. Knowledge is going to leapfrog this layer entirely, and land even further from private experience. Plato relegates these things to the realm of mere belief, apparently on the grounds that they change, but why? I can know that I have flowers in my room, what kind they are, and indeed how long they are likely to last, although all the time they are changing. The prejudice against the ordinary world seems to come from nowhere, or perhaps as Nietzsche thought, from some deep hatred of ordinary life.

When we finally do come to the realm of knowledge, we meet the distinction between geometry done by means of diagrams and geometry done with no recourse to diagrams but purely mathematically. The first, it is implied, is interesting enough, and gives us a kind of knowledge of an inferior variety. But the fourth is the real thing: circles and right-angled triangles, squares and polygons, in all their unchanging, glorious abstraction. However, there is still no hint of how to deploy the exalted status of mathematical objects in any practical way – in the world of ethics or politics, for example.

So the image of the line is more confusing than enlightening, and we turn to Book VII of *Republic*, and the most famous metaphor in the history of philosophy – the resonant allegory that everyone remembers, and that even people with minimal exposure to philosophy itself have probably heard of: the Myth of the Cave.

In this fantastic image the plight of ordinary, uneducated, unenlightened humanity is compared to that of prisoners in a cave. It is a rather peculiar cave, however. They are tied so as only to see the back wall of the cave. Matters are arranged so that behind their backs is a fire, and a kind of roadway along which are carried all sorts of statuettes and animal models, puppets or marionettes. The fire casts the shadow of these artificial things on to the wall the prisoners see: 'the shadows of artefacts... constitute the only reality people in this situation would recognize'.

Ascent from the cave happens when one of the prisoners is released, and made to turn and see the marionettes themselves, and the fire. This unfamiliar sight would frighten and bewilder him, habituated as he is to the world of shadows (in terms of the line he has now reached the second of the four stages). Further ascent takes the ex-prisoner up 'a rough steep slope' to the world of daylight, which again is unfamiliar and overwhelming. Gradually, however, he would begin to make out the real things of everyday life (now apparently corresponding to the third section of the line rather than the second). And then, the last thing he would do is to make out the heavenly bodies and the sun itself, 'not the displaced image of the sun in water or elsewhere, but the sun on its own, in its proper place'. This is the pinnacle of understanding, the last illumination, an acquaintance with the Form of the Good itself. Whatever that may be.

Perhaps the power of this tremendous allegory is directly proportional to its lack of specificity. Just as with the initial distinction between knowledge and its domain, versus belief and its domain, or with the image of the line, it is far from clear how to interpret the ascent Plato demands, or the procedures of education or illumination that would further it. European and Islamic thought has generally followed one of three broad models.

CHAPTER 11

The Religious Interpretation

Now, what we are dealing with here, it would seem, is… the reorientation of a mind from a kind of twilight to true daylight – and this reorientation is an ascent to reality, or in other words true philosophy. (VII, 521c)

The first model of ascent is seriously transcendental. It contrasts this world with that which is to come, or rather, that which is available to the elect. It takes seriously St Paul's admonition in 1 Corinthians 13:12, that 'now we see through a glass, darkly; but then face to face'. On this view Plato did pretty well, in fact about as well as someone who was not given the Christian revelation could do, by way of understanding the illumination offered by ascent to the transcendental world. This is the Plato transmitted to Europe by so-called 'middle Platonists' such as the contemporary of Christ, Philo of Alexandria (Philo Judaeus), then further by Plotinus in the second century, and that became folded into Christianity, notably by Augustine and Boethius, in the fourth and fifth centuries. It is the Plato of the Renaissance philosopher Marsilio Ficino, who was president of Lorenzo de Medici's Florentine Academy and believed that Plato should be preached in the churches of Florence alongside the Bible. It is Plato of the so-called 'Cambridge Platonists' of the seventeenth century, a group of Cambridge theologians and philosophers looking for a bulwark against the rising tide of science and secularism (represented by Hobbes). It is usually described as 'Neoplatonism', but that is a recent categorization, and the Neoplatonists thought of themselves as no more than good Platonists. It was, however, Plato interpreted as offering a cosmology, an account of the entire structure of creation. In it, the Form of the Good becomes the creating and sustaining power at the centre of the universe, the eternal and unchanging source of energy and light. Below this pinnacle are successive 'hypostases' or levels of creation. *Logos* is one of them. It is the Word, the creative power expressed in law, the guiding principle of the cosmos and so in effect God's Word, the instrument of creation. It gives the underlying forms or archetypes behind the visible world, and this in turn affords us only a shadow far removed from them. Poor old matter and humanity, as contaminated with material existence, come very low in the ladder of creation.

A first-century Jewish philosopher from Alexandria, Philo Judaeus, is pivotal in the assimilation of Platonism and Christianity, and not only Christianity but Judaism and later Islam. For Philo, God is almost totally unknowable, indeed unnameable and beyond comprehension by ideas. The relation between human beings and God therefore needs mediation, and here *logos* or the Word functions as the intermediary, parallel to Plato's world of Forms or arche-types, allowing the adept at least an ascent towards the inaccessible pinnacle of unity with God. Philo allowed himself allegorical interpretations of the Judaic scriptures, bringing their message as closely as possible into harmony with this version of the Platonic worldview. Platonism thereby became the background philosophical underpinning of the theologies of the monotheistic religions.

This role is handsomely acknowledged by Augustine, who thought that Platonists had some conception of God as the 'cause of existence, the principle of reason and the rule of life' – all things grasped by the initiate who has finally seen the Sun.[1] Augustine was joined by other churchmen who thought that Plato was 'but Moses in Attic Greek', and clearly regretted that they had not been around to baptize him. He was, unfortunately, denied the Christian revelation (and the Judaic and Islamic versions). But Platonists, it was felt, could have become Christians with the change of a few words and phrases.

Not that all was sweetness and light. For while it may have suited the theologians of Christianity to make Platonism into its backbone, the cracks in this unity are actually all too apparent. The eternal principle of Plato and Plotinus is not the caring, all-too-human, God of Judaism and Christianity, which itself is a magnification of human emotions such as love or pity, or in fiercer versions, anger and jealousy. It is more a principle than a person, an impersonal source of the cosmos. It is not a fatherly, caring, all-too-human creator. It could not conceivably itself become incarnate. So in the way of things, Christianity eventually decided it could defeat Platonism, and conceal its theological debt to it. The congregations did not need Plotinus's abstract principle of illumination. They did not want an illumination reserved for those who have studied mathematics for ten years and dialectic for five. They wanted consolation, forgiveness, a target for intercessionary prayer, and the other emotional props and indulgences of popular religion. The leaders wanted to feed their own watchdogs of guilt and sin, and the profitable monopoly they enjoyed on the search for redemption. At almost the same time as Augustine was composing *The City of God*, the Christian patriarch of Alexandria, Cyril, egged his flock on to murder the Neoplatonist and mathematician Hypatia, an act which contributed to his acceptance as a Doctor of the Church by Leo XIII in 1883. It took a very elevated mind to reconcile paganism and the Church, and no popular religion can flourish by privileging the elevated mind.

As a generalization, we could say that Plato's transcendentalism appeals to people who feel themselves to be strangers in this world. The first sentence of Porphyry's life of his teacher, Plotinus, tells us that Plotinus seemed to be someone ashamed of being in a body. Indeed, this shame was the core of the Platonic rejection of Christianity, which it otherwise closely resembles. As Porphyry forcibly put it: 'How can we admit that the divine became an embryo, and that after its birth, it was wrapped up in swaddling clothes, covered with blood, bile, and even worse things?' But in either its Christian or its more abstract, more elevated Platonic form the thought that the soul is only accidentally, and temporarily, burdened with the mess, pain and appetites of bodily existence can be both a consolation and a spur to asceticism, to withdrawal from worldly concerns into private contemplation. If this contemplation is also interpreted as unity with the divine, acquaintance with the principle underlying the whole cosmos, so much the better.

Naturally there is a problem, in this kind of theology as in others, for why the eternal principle, itself wholly good, should be responsible for a world, or descending succession of worlds, many of which are not at all good. Indeed, Christians found here a point of counter-attack against Neoplatonists: why would souls which had once inhabited the eternal world, the court of the king, leave such a blessed place and seek out 'these terrestrial parts where they inhabit opaque bodies, intimately mixed with blood and humours, in sacks of excrement and unspeakable pots of urine'?[2] It was not particularly strong ground on which to fight, since Christianity has exactly the same problem, of reconciling a world of sacks of excrement and the rest with the benevolent rule of an omnipotent and loving God. And Neoplatonists found a 'reason', if such vocabulary can be applied to something eternal and unchanging, for the principle of the cosmos to have issued in a universe with an admixture of imperfection. Not to have done so would have disrupted the principle that non-existence is the ultimate evil, so that whatever goodness could be responsible for, it must of necessity create. In human terms, anything else would argue 'envy' or a kind of mean spirit. Elaborated upon, this idea became that of the 'Great Chain of Being', the idea that the universe was a plenitude of every kind of possible created thing, from the highest to the lowest.[3]

In this picture, we are in the Cave at the beginning because of the fallen (physical, embodied) state of humanity. To begin the ascent out may take one's own effort of will, properly directed by God's word, or may represent an arbitrary act of God's good grace. Either way the 'rough steep slope' to the world of sunlight becomes equated with salvation, and especially with a triumph over the body, conceived of as the locus of sensory pleasure, pain, desire, fear and suffering, sin and temptation. The final illumination, which for Plato is the triumph of understanding, reason and intelligence, is subtly reconfigured as the triumph of the purely 'spiritual' element of the soul, either temporarily, as in moments of mystical illumination, or permanently, as in salvation after bodily death.

From Plotinus through to adepts such as the early twentieth-century French philosopher Henri Bergson, the religious Plato has consorted with the idea of mystical awareness of transcendence, an awareness, however, that is often achieved by a dark journey into the centre of the soul. By confronting the self and what it is, the adept gains freedom from its demands. The idea suggests a purely personal struggle, not a passive reception of doctrine, such as might be transmitted by a Church or a book. In turn, this explains why 'dead' Aristotelian logic was more associated with the Catholic

Church, while Plato remains the champion of inner-light Protestantism whereby each pilgrim is responsible for his or her own salvation.

This idea in turn has affinities with another doctrine of Plato's, albeit one more associated with another dialogue, *Meno*. Here Plato suggests that our innate knowledge is in fact a recollection of knowledge (not belief) gained in a previous state of existence, before birth. Christianity could not absorb that as it stands, since it denies the pre-existence of souls. But the doctrine could be tamed, as it were, into the belief that there is an 'inner candle of the Lord', a source of light within each of us, a private Platonic sun, visible after a path of redemption and purification.[4] Recollection was much used, but similarly tamed, later on in England in the eighteenth century by the poets Coleridge, Shelley and Wordsworth. Each was enchanted by the idea of 'the eclipsing curse of birth' which permeated Wordsworth's many celebrations of childhood, and especially his 'Ode on the Intimations of Immortality', although probably each regarded it more as a charming idea than as a doctrine.[5] It was sufficiently vague (but uplifting) to incorporate both a sentimental conception of childish innocence and the apparently conflicting view that innocence is not, as it might seem, mere ignorance, but itself a kind of superior knowledge, a recollection of transcendence such as the Platonic philosopher might possess, or the soul might look forward to re-establishing in eternity. Such an idea may be food for the poet, but it is not exactly a belief to which one could really assent.

The transcendental interpretation may have inspired religious minds, but it also draws the venom of philosophers
who are not estranged from the world, and who despise
those who are. The elevated mysticism of Plotinus is only to
some tastes, and in any case it easily degenerates into mere
transcendental twaddle, or the mumbo-jumbo and charla-
tanry of hermeticists, theosophists and other cultists. So far
as Plato goes, however, the central problems are first that
there is not a very close resemblance between the kind of
education necessary for the Platonic elite, and the mystical
illumination celebrated by the ascetic sage or saint who
has turned his back on the world and the intellect alike.
Whatever else the Platonic education demands, it clearly
requires a deep immersion in mathematics and in dialectic or
reason (and partly for military purposes, as is clear in VII,
525c). It is essentially an intellectual journey, although built
on the foundation of a childhood steeped in harmony and
proportion.

Second, there is the even more pressing problem of why
anyone takes the reverse journey. Plato is clear that the
philosopher, having exited from the Cave, must return and
'apply' his revelation to the business of governing the state.
The question is, why should he do so, and still more, what has
he discovered that qualifies him to do so? Plato is aware of
this as a problem, of course. At VI, 500b, he insists on it:

> The point is, of course, Adeimantus, that someone whose
> mind really is fixed on reality has no time to cast his gaze

downwards on to the affairs of men and to enter into their disputes (and so be infected with resentment and malice).

So long as the emphasis is on transcending the worldly, this problem can have no answer. Perhaps it is fascinating enough, and even 'revelatory' of something, to contemplate the eternal and unchanging. But we still have no model for applying that unchanging and unvarying reality to the world of military tactics, politics and business, the world of resentment and malice. Why, then, return to the Cave, and what in any case do you bring with you? The Christian hermit contemplating his skull may have a sage and 'philosophical' attitude to mortal life and its problems, but he is scarcely a model for the well-ordered ruler of the state, even if we manage to tolerate or admire him on his own terms.

CHAPTER 12

The Poetic Interpretation

> *Can you find any flaw, then, in an occupation like this, which*
> *in order to be competently practised requires the following*
> *inherent qualities in a person: a good memory, quickness at*
> *learning, broadness of vision, elegance, and love of and*
> *affiliation to truth, morality, courage, and self-discipline?*
> (VI, 487a)

Hence there is space for the second interpretation that captured the European imagination and which went in a very different direction. This also took seriously material from other dialogues, this time *Phaedrus* and *Symposium*. It brings to the foreground something surprisingly absent in the central books of *Republic*, which is the importance of beauty and the related importance of love or *eros* in Plato's metaphor of ascent. In *Symposium*, Socrates (on the face of it a much more attractive Socrates than his namesake in *Republic*) relates how he learned a story of ascent from a wise old priestess, Diotima. Her ascent of the soul begins from the experience of beauty, in the person of someone who is loved. It progresses, of course, from love of corporeal to spiritual beauty, or from beauty embodied in one person to that which is visible in many. But – and here is the difference from the religious interpretation – the initial beauty of the individual is never wholly left behind. Such beauty is itself divine bounty. It is always to be seen. It is not the beginning of an ascent to anything unseen, although it may be the beginning of an ascent to a different, better appreciation of what is seen. There is no lament here for what Coleridge, enamoured of the transcendental interpretation, denigrated as 'the despotism of the eye'.[1]

This is the Plato that is most attractive to artists and creators. The idea is that to look on things with real love is already to discern immortal qualities in them – qualities of beauty, grace, truth or harmony, that can in principle be manifested anywhere in space or time and are in that sense timeless. The paradigm Platonic experience is not now otherworldly, but this-worldly, only this world appreciated as it should be, when the banquet of the senses is enlarged with imagination and insight. Frequently, the insight is supposed to have a moral dimension. In the works of the writer Iris Murdoch, for example, the connection with ethics is made because the experience of love takes the agent outside him or herself, making possible an appreciation of the beloved that is itself an 'unselfing', representing a displacement of the selfish ego from its usual throne in the centre of things.

This view has much to commend it. It makes excellent sense of the evident connection in Plato's mind between beauty, goodness and truth. For us, perhaps, these three have little to do with each other. Beauty, if we talk about it at all, is relegated to the peripheral, and persons who harp on it are regarded with suspicion: airy-fairy aesthetes, weightless and unserious. Goodness is a matter of ethics, and while we ourselves may have principles which raise us above the Athenian envoys, we become nervous if it intrudes too far into people's minds. 'Do-gooder' is a derogatory term. Meanwhile our paradigm of truth is probably scientific truth, which has nothing much to do with either beauty or goodness. As in the Humean model of motivation and action outlined above, we tend to think that knowledge is one thing, and how you choose to use it, for good or ill, to create beauty or destroy it, is another thing altogether. Indeed, Plato also recognizes that the lower forms of belief and perhaps knowledge are at the disposal of twisted ends just as much as higher ends (VII, 519a). The connection between knowledge or understanding and goodness is only forged, if it ever is, at the highest level.

Part of the charm of Plato is the sense of being in a world in which these fractures did not exist. Ours may be a world in which there is a division between fact on the one hand, and value on the other. But his world is, in the phrase of the godfather of modern sociology, Max Weber, an enchanted world, in which ideas like proportion and harmony efface any such division. Beauty makes both goodness and truth manifest, so its perception and the love it engenders together give us the first step out of the Cave. Beauty is the first erasure of the distinction between fact and value. It is borne in upon us, in erotic experience, like facts. But it is intrinsically or essentially connected with the values of pleasure and love. And just as it erases the fact-value distinction, so beauty erases the tyranny of the self. In loving something or someone for beauty's sake we are, as Iris Murdoch says, 'unselfed'. Selfish desire has no place in the pure aesthetic experience.

The poetic Plato is the prophet of courtly love, of pure, spiritual unity with the beloved, contrasted with the sweaty appetites of the unwashed. He is the Plato of the first part of John Donne's 'Ecstasy':

> Our hands were firmly cemented
>> With a fast balm, which thence did spring
> Our eye-beams twisted, and did thread
>> Our eyes, upon one double string;
>
> …
>
> As, 'twixt two equal armies, Fate
>> Suspends uncertain victory,
> Our souls, (which to advance their state,
>> Were gone out), hung 'twixt her, and me.
>
> And whilst our souls negotiate there,
>> We like sepulchral statues lay;
> All day, the same our postures were,
>> And we said nothing, all the day.

Notice that an afternoon gazing into the beloved's eyes is not a substitution of the otherworldly for the specific here and now. On the contrary, it is an intense, almost microscopic appreciation of the here and now: one illuminated by the sun,

as it were, rather than in the gloom. Donne himself is, however, an imperfect Platonist of this stamp, since while all this
commingling of souls is fine enough, it becomes, dare one
suppose, a little tedious, and Donne is content that the body
should eventually have its say as well:

> But O alas, so long, so far
>   Our bodies why do we forbear?
> They are ours, though they are not we, we are
>   The intelligences, they the sphere.
>
> …
>
> So must pure lovers' souls descend
>   T' affections, and to faculties,
> Which sense may reach and apprehend,
> Else a great prince in prison lies.

Although this lapse may, after all, be a true rendering of Plato
himself, to whom return to the Cave and to the world of the
senses and their illusions is not entirely a fall, but a natural
progress.

The distinction between the religious Plato and the poetic
one is extremely apt to blur. In one respect the poetic Plato is
actually nearer to one strand in Christianity. The poetic
Plato's beauty can be incarnated – that is its whole point – and
similarly according to Christianity the good itself can be
incarnated, and once was. Each philosophy needs to effect a
bridge between something which is too rarefied, too abstract,

too pure, to engage with human life, and something else which can find a seat in day-to-day living. For the poetic Platonist the soul is revivified by a renewed erotic perception of beauty; for the Christian by a renewed acquaintance with the personification of goodness in the incarnation of Christ.

For Christianity this is, however, just one element in a fundamentally otherworldly philosophy. Christ is himself just a signpost to the real consummation of eternal life, in the other world. For the poetic Platonist, the incarnation is everything.

The problem of the return to the Cave is not so severe for poetic Platonism as for religious Platonism. But it does not disappear entirely, either. It is not so much the rediscovery of the body that is a problem, as a rediscovery of pursuits and problems that have nothing much to do with beauty or love: problems of politics and morals, for instance. With respect to Iris Murdoch, we may yet doubt if the Melians would have been impressed if the Athenian envoys had come ashore while raptly admiring the line of beauty incarnated in a rose-leaf, or the beauty of their toy-boys' profiles. The suggestion must be that so much immersion in beauty would free the Athenians from the ambition, fear or greed that prompted their brutal politics. But amongst human beings, this is not how it works. The aesthetic only forms a temporary respite from the moral and political. The Athenian envoys, however susceptible to beauty they might have been, would soon enough have cast aside their roseleaves and toy-boys, and got to work blackmailing the Melians, just as they in fact did. The lives of the artists are seldom all that edifying. And that in turn reminds us that while the themes of love and beauty are prominent, as we have said, in other dialogues, in *Republic* itself they are overshadowed by the eventual banishment of the artists, to which we shortly return. As the quotation at the head of this section shows, Plato seems to be pursuing themes other than contemplative immersion in beauty. An enjoyable afternoon lying on the river bank with a lover, or raptly engaging with the exhibits in a gallery, can scarcely be said to require each or any of 'a good memory, quickness at learning, broadness of vision, elegance, and love of and affiliation to truth, morality, courage, and self-discipline' which his philosopher-king must exhibit. So in spite of the enchantments of the poetic life, we still lack a satisfactory model for the ascent from the Cave.

CHAPTER 13

The Scientific
Interpretation

*'It's nothing special', I said. 'It's the ability to distinguish
one, two, and three – in short, I'm talking about number and
counting. I mean, isn't it the case that every branch of expertise
and knowledge is bound to have some involvement with
numbers and with counting?'* (VII, 522c)

The third interpretation of the Myth of the Cave takes
seriously Plato's talk of order and proportion, as well as the
timelessness of the reality with which the elite is acquainted.
The suggestion is that the transcendental world is
fundamentally that of mathematics, or at most the world of
mathematical objects suitably extended, to include,
inevitably, the good and the beautiful.

It is almost impossible to over-emphasize the place that
mathematics, particularly the theory of harmony and the
theory of geometry, occupied in Plato's conception of
wisdom, or insight into the scheme of the cosmos. Plato is
supposed to have visited southern Italy, and learned what he
could from the Pythagoreans installed at their base there in
Metapontum, on the Gulf of Taranto. To these the whole

universe ran according to a mathematical scheme, just as the sequence of musical notes obeyed the mathematical laws of harmony. Plato's description of the education of the elite flows from mathematics (VII, 525a–531d).

The mathematical model makes a good deal of sense. The subject-matter of arithmetic and geometry is timeless. Furthermore, the understanding we attain by using them is often timeless as well: the laws governing musical harmony, for instance. Better than that, we find here for the first time a kind of defence of the view which I pilloried in chapter 9, that the domains of knowledge and belief are different, and that the first concerns what is permanent and unvarying while the second does not. Suppose we think not in terms of *knowledge* but of *understanding*. Then there is something right about the claim that however often we are faced with change, we only come to understand it by bringing to bear something unchanging, a constant that can be seen throughout the process, or that can be brought up alongside it, like a ruler, in order to make it intelligible. And perhaps this is the vital nerve of Plato's system.

Thus faced with a changing system, science itself requires the application of laws, themselves unchanging, governing the changes of the magnitudes defining the system, and its state at one time and another. These laws, and an initial set of magnitudes, govern the state of the system at a later time. What is fixed may be mass, or temperature, or energy, or combinations of these or complex functions of them, or even more ethereal quantities such as probabilities. But something there must be, to feed the equations that describe the evolution of state – the nature of changes in systems, whether they are mechanical, chemical, gravitational, thermodynamic, or quantum-mechanical – and thence make scientific understanding of change possible. Where one constant after another flickers out, for example as we consider times nearer and nearer to the 'singularity' which we dub the big bang, we get closer and closer to the point at which our understanding gives out as well.

On this account, it is the scientist and mathematician who 'sees eternity in a wild flower' – or in the starry night sky, or the intricacies of the atom – by finding the changeless laws or forms of growth underlying temporal becoming. It would of course be entirely unhistorical to credit the Pythagoreans, or Plato himself, with an understanding of the shape that scientific explanation would eventually take. Even late into the seventeenth century, when scientists such as Newton were finally coming up with equations governing simple mechanical and gravitational interactions, the prevailing view was that this was all very well, but it did not really amount to 'science', the holy grail of rational, mathematical insight into not just the way things are, but the way they have to be. It was only in the eighteenth century that philosophers reconciled themselves to the empiricist dispensation, that the kind of thing Newton did was all we were ever going to get. It would be absurd to see Plato as anticipating those centuries. But all that we really require for this kind of interpretation of the enlightenment of the philosopher is that Plato and

Pythagoras knew they were 'on to something', so that the triumph represented by a mathematical modelling of musical harmony was a paradigm to follow. Hence the massive concentration upon mathematics in the education of the elite, in the ideal republic.

The mathematical/scientific model has another advantage. Modern epistemologists fall over themselves denouncing the 'spectator theory of knowledge', or the view that they find in Plato which thinks of moments of especially intense vision ('illuminations') as the best exemplars of knowledge. But in Plato (and still more obviously in Aristotle) the relevant 'spectator' is not what Plato would have called a mere sightseer, but rather what we would call the theorist: the person who can deploy an understanding of what he sees and thereby literally sees something different from the untutored eye, however intense the latter may be. In fact, the Greek word *theoria* originally meant a spectator or spectacle in the rather refined context of the expert or official observer of a sacred event: someone who understands what is going on (compare the expert spectator of a cricket match, or the expert listener to a jazz quartet, beside the casual sightseer or listener).[1]

It may well be that Plato himself conceived the application of mathematics to nature in a more exotic way than any gained by measuring magnitude of different properties of systems, and establishing by observation and conjecture, trial and error, how they change through time. He probably had something much more occult and 'mystical' in mind, like persons fascinated by numerology, cryptic understandings, golden sections, Fibonacci series, and the mathematics of prime numbers. He can hardly have had our own post-Kantian understanding of the distinction between applied and pure mathematics, or in other words between the brute empirical fact and the purely a priori abstract structures of numbers and sets. Francis Bacon, quoted in the Introduction, clearly saw it that way, regarding Plato as having 'contaminated and corrupted' any chance of Greek natural science by an admixture of speculation and theology, whereas only the revolution he was himself advocating would find the right mix:

> Those who have treated of the sciences have been either empiricists or dogmatists. Empiricists, like ants, simply accumulate and use; Rationalists, like spiders, spin webs from themselves; the way of the bee is in between: it takes material from the flowers of the garden and the field; but it has the ability to convert and digest them.[2]

However, a more positive spin can be put on *Republic* than Bacon suggests. It clearly envisages the use of mathematics for military matters, but also for the theory of music and of astronomy (VII, 530b), and these subjects might conform to 'the way of the bee'. Apart from that it offers two central examples of mathematics in action in Plato's mind, and unfortunately they are less reassuring. At VIII, 546, he is explaining how even a well-ordered community ruled by philosopher-kings could degenerate. This could happen because one of the rulers' prime responsibilities is to time the conception and births of children. An elaborate foray into the mathematics of cubes, diagonals, harmonies, and so forth produces the so-called 'nuptial number' or 12, 960,000, although what that has to do with the timing of births remains entirely obscure. However, if the guardians are unaware of this number and its application, they 'pair men and women sexually on the wrong occasions' and the culture spirals downwards. Plato's reasoning was proverbially incomprehensible, even in antiquity, and moderns have to confess pretty much total bafflement.[3] The impression, certainly, is of a Pythagorean confidence that the laws relating to numbers also govern the universe, and then that sufficient knowledge of those laws, and perhaps skill in applying them, will enable the wise to order things. In this case what they are ordering is the eugenic policy of the society. But it is unintelligent for us to let our sense of revulsion at this destroy our admiration for the fact that Pythagoreans and Plato were indeed on to something. They were on to the mathematicization of nature, the discovery of properties and relations that can be ordered by magnitude, generating data that, once fed into the right (eternal) equations, determine how things fall out. Plato's eugenic application may be mysterious, and fanciful, and perhaps partakes more of astrology than astronomy. But the ambition may have been wholly laudable.

The other exercise in mathematics, in a lighter vein, occurs at IX, 587e. Here Plato is calculating how much happier a philosopher-king must be than a dictator. By assuming three kinds of ruler, and three kinds of pleasure, with the philosopher at the top and the dictator and his pleasures at the bottom, Plato comes up with the figure of 729 (9^3 or 3^6) as the ratio of a philosopher's happiness to that of a dictator. Again, there seems to be a misdirected enthusiasm for the spurious appearance of accuracy and 'science' that numbers provide in contexts such as this. But Plato was neither the first nor the last to fall into this particular trap. The philosopher Jeremy Bentham's notorious 'felicific calculus' was just a generalization of the idea, and arguably substantial parts of the discipline of welfare economics is a temple to it. In fact, it remains a difficult logical exercise to tease out exactly the properties which enable us to provide a scale, either ordering magnitudes or doing the more exacting job of associating cardinal numbers with them. Pleasure is probably more like 'hardness', which can be ordered (on the Moh scale of minerals, hardness is indexed from 1 to 10, according to whether the substance in questions scratches or is scratched by comparison substances) but not assigned magnitudes among which arithmetical ratios make any sense. It makes no sense to say that topaz is twice as hard as quartz for example. In *Republic* the mathematical ratio of the philosopher's pleasure to the dictator's may be offered somewhat tongue-in-cheek, while the first, eugenic exercise, seems to have been entirely serious.

The obvious advantage of the mathematical/scientific interpretation of the ascent from the Cave is that it accords with the pre-eminent place of mathematics in the education of the philosopher-king. The ruler is not given a spiritual training in religious mysticism. Nor is he given a Romantic development saturated in poetry and imagination – on the contrary, these are to be banished from the well-ordered state and hence by analogy, from the well-ordered mind. Instead, he or she, having been proved exceptional in the years of primary education and military training, up to around age twenty, is then offered ten years of mathematics, followed by five years of dialectic or logic: the kind of immersion in argument that the liberal Socrates of the earlier dialogues represents. Mathematics is near the copestone of the Platonic arch. Naturally, philosophy has that honour. But mathematics is certainly the supporting intellectual buttress.

There are other pleasant features of this interpretation. One is that Plato often associates the fact that the world is changing with the fact that people come to different opinions about it, as two very similar obstacles to understanding (e.g. V, 479a–d). At first sight this is puzzling. Change is one thing, but the different perspectives different witnesses may take on what things are like, whether they are big or small, sweet or sour, and so on, is quite another thing. Again, however, science gives us a useful entrée into this aspect of Plato's thought. It transcends relativity, not by going off to discuss something else entirely, but by finding what is invariant behind the different judgements. The perspective according to which the finger is bigger than the moon, and that according to which the moon is bigger than a finger, are alike intelligible in terms of different points of view on the one invariant set of spatial relations.[4] We come to understand different perspectives, when we do, not by succumbing to the relativistic idea of utterly incommensurable verdicts, made by people living in separate worlds, but by finding what is invariant, and therefore explains the emergence of difference itself.

Relativism in judgement can be comprehended by distinguishing the invariant way in which the one reality acts upon observers who themselves occupy different places or times or who have different senses or different historical and cultural experiences. The theory of relativity itself substitutes one invariance (distance in space-time) for two magnitudes hitherto thought invariant (distance in space, distance in time) but which prove to vary with the velocity of the observer. That is progress, and in broad outline it follows what we said about the scientific understanding of change. We comprehend variety in judgement, just as we comprehend change, by finding solid rock under the shifting sands.

The other, even more important feature is that this interpretation solves the problem of relevance. As we have seen in the previous two chapters, on more transcendental, otherworldly, interpretations of what is required, there is the severe problem of getting back to earth. How should knowledge of another world qualify one to behave well, govern well, or indeed have anything at all to do with this one? It is fine to see eternity in a wild flower, but what if that amounts to seeing eternity instead of the wild flower? That is not much use to the herbalist or horticulturalist. On the scientific model, the answer is immediate. The scientist alone understands the unchanging within the changing. He alone is not a mere 'sightseer' or theatre-goer. But he does not see the unchanging *instead* of the changing. He sees the growth and decay of this actual flower, here, now, in front of him, but *in the light of* known constancies. For this reason he can predict and explain what happens to this very flower. His knowledge is not other-worldly, but this-worldly – yet it goes beyond that of the mere sightseer.

Where the mathematical-scientific model breaks down is, of course, with the final five years of dialectic, equipping the philosopher with the kind of understanding of men and events that entitle him or her to govern. As VII, 519a, reminds us, most knowledge may be used for good or ill, and that is certainly true of scientific knowledge. The final illumination somehow transcends that limitation. It is easy to feel that it has to be something beatific: a vision in as much as, like sight, it generates understanding and 'oneness' with the order of nature, and beatific in that once achieved it guarantees the goodness of the subject who has gained it. But we are not told how. If Hume is right, we can never be told how, since the idea of a state of mind which counts both as some kind of understanding of things, and also and at the same time one which of necessity points its subject towards the good and away from the bad, is a delusion. Noble perhaps, but a delusion none the less. Also, unfortunately, a profoundly dangerous delusion, substituting as it does an illumination open only to the elite, and incommunicable to the vulgar, for anything more ordinary. In this it belittles the human, democratic, shared processes of communicating, decreasing fear and mistrust, increasing humanity, and enlarging sympathy – the actual routes through which moral improvement emerges.

Do we want to settle for just one of the religious, the poetical, and the mathematical-scientific interpretations of the Myth of the Cave? I do not think so. Like other myths it weaves its own spell, and is sufficiently capacious to include almost any journey of increased understanding, whatever local form it may take. This is, of course, part of its power, but also part of what may make it dangerous.

CHAPTER 14

Disorderly Cities;
Disorderly People

> *'If one type of character outweighs the rest, so to speak, then
> don't you think it draws all the other types with it?'*
>
> *'Yes, that's the only possible way in which political systems
> arise,' he agreed.* (VIII, 544e)

After chewing the heavy metaphysical and epistemological
themes of Books V to VII, it is something of a relief to return to
a diet of Plato-lite in Book VIII. It is not that the heavy themes
are entirely forgotten. But for the moment the precise nature
of the illumination or understanding obtained by the philosopher-kings is less important than the lovingly painted canvas
of folly- and vice-displaying kings who are not philosophers.
Nobody can read Book VIII without recognizing that Plato
was a connoisseur of human flaws and failures, a worthy
ancestor of Swift, Voltaire, Pope or Proust.

There is one interesting aspect of this book to notice before
we come to the display itself. Plato makes it clear that he goes
further than the analogy between the city and the soul or
agent that has been important so far. He believes in a causal
connection rather than a mere analogy. As the quotation

above shows, he thinks that it is the nature of agents that determines the nature of the political collective that they form.

At first glance this might seem innocuous enough. We would expect, for instance, a warlike society to come about as a result of warlike individual members. Anything else might seem almost miraculous, as if a collective composed entirely of pacifists could in some other unnatural way itself be warlike. But in fact the matter is much more complex. Indeed, there exists no accepted taxonomy of the ways in which properties of collectives arise from (in philosopher's jargon 'supervene upon') the properties of individual members. It is easy to think of exceptions to the simple model in which warlike individuals generate warlike society. One divergence arises when in public discourse certain kinds of interest become inadmissible. The individuals in a tribunal may then individually desire one kind of outcome, but by the constraints of their role be unable either to advocate it or to implement it. In the United States, for example, each member of a Supreme Court might be a devout Christian, but the Court itself may be unable to make a decision that would be welcome to people of that particular religion. Such an optimistic complication lies at the very heart of constitutional design, whereby through a suitable system of checks and balances the energies of people who are individually self-seeking and partisan can, it is hoped, be harnessed towards collective ends.

A similar role may be played by the culture of honour, or

Locke's law of fashion or Grote's King Nomos from chapter 1. Here a set of individually self-seeking agents may find themselves constrained in their pursuit of their own interest by a sense of what is and what is not 'done', which is itself the creature of their collective interactions and expectations. So as well as warlike individuals making up a warlike society, we have to recognize the reverse direction of causation, where a warlike society makes warlike individuals.

A more pessimistic dissonance arises when individuals who are themselves perfectly rational become enmeshed in versions of the voting paradox first noticed by Condorcet in the eighteenth century. In the simplest version we have three people (A, B and C) ranking three upshots, X, Y and Z. A prefers X to Y to Z. B prefers Y to Z to X. Finally C prefers Z to X to Y. Then a majority of two out of three rank X above Y; a majority of two out of three rank Y above Z, and if X outranks Y and Y outranks Z, we would expect X to outrank Z. But alas, a majority of two out of three also rank Z above X. Taken together, these rankings are incoherent, and the collective may be paralysed in deciding what to do. Yet each individual agent is perfectly coherent, so once more the collective is only an impure mirror of the individuals who make it up.

Plato shows no awareness of the complexities of supervenience, and historically one cannot blame him. He clung to the simple model whereby the follies and vices of particular states would arise from, but also display, writ large as it were, the follies and vices of the individuals making them up. Given the indefinite but vast number of ways in which individuals can shake up their own cocktails of vice and folly, it might seem a long and dreary business to begin to catalogue them all. But Plato has a brisk set of categories, and a sprightly brush when it comes to painting the way they play out in politics and individuals alike.

The five systems that interest Plato are first, of course, the rule of the philosopher-kings: the particular kind of aristocratic system that he has been fashioning all along. Second there is the rule of the 'spirited' kind of aristocracy, a Spartan or heroic system marked by competition and determination. Plato calls this a 'timocracy', or 'timarchy', deriving from rule by ambition. Third there is oligarchy, by which Plato means plutocracy, or rule by the rich. Fourth there is democracy, or rule by the people, and fifth there is absolute dictatorship, rule by one tyrant. These systems form a descending staircase, and by showing us the descent Plato hopes to convince us to admire the rule of philosopher-kings, and the psychology of the philosophers themselves.

Timarchy is the system found in Sparta. The timarchic individual resembles the man of too much *thumos* whom we met in section 7 – tough, brave, mettlesome and stupid. A system in which such individuals rule shares the military aspects of life in the ideal republic. Its militia will live the same communal life, and there is a similar emphasis on war as the proper employment of the ruling class. However, there will be overvaluation of military men, and because of the general loutishness of the society, there will be greed, and since displays of wealth are frowned upon, this greed will issue in miserliness. Individuals within the society will be supercilious, harsh but submissive to authority, ambitious but free from the controls offered by reason and culture. They will come about as a degeneration from philosopher-kings, largely because philosopher-kings will be undervalued by women and servants, inferior people, who will be unable to appreciate their reserve and unworldliness. They will set other values against them, and eventually these other values will triumph (one might think of the declining status of professors, and of academic virtues in general, in our own body politic).

The oligarchic system descends from timarchy rather as the values of professional sport change from those of sheer glory in competition to those accorded to unseemly displays of wealth. This in turn breeds envy, and once more a corresponding undervaluation of genuine virtue. The rulers of a timarchy then scheme to make wealth a necessary condition of participation in public office, as we see in the USA. Gradually their increasingly mercenary natures unfit them for martial pursuits, even making them unwilling to pay a tax so that others fight for them (which in any event breeds fear and conflict within the state). Furthermore the oligarch, by capitalizing on his wealth, can become a mere consumer, a drone without a purposeful role in his society.[1] Finally, since society divides into the haves and the have-nots, we get antagonism and plots, beggars and criminals.

An oligarchic individual descends from a timarchic individual who has been ruined. He feels the sting of poverty, and installs his 'desirous and mercenary' side on the throne of his concerns (VIII, 553c). He is then led by greed and miserliness, although not so much by appetite. In fact, he is rather ascetic, since unnecessary desires cost money pointlessly. However, he will find criminal desires within himself, when opportunities for fraud or theft arise, and even if these are suppressed by fear of discovery or the remnants of decency, this itself will be a conflict within his soul, corresponding to the conflicts in the oligarchic city. His meanness is a faultline of weakness, interfering with his capacity to earn prestige or honour. He is a failure.

The transition to the penultimate system, democracy, happens when oligarchy has had its day. The oligarchs will breed indisciplined and intemperate children, spoiled, soft and lazy, many of whom will ruin themselves. These become resentful and envious, but this goes unnoticed by the rich who remain blind to the evil their pursuit of wealth creates. When a crisis comes, such as a war, the poor get a taste of their own power and become aware of the flaccid condition of the rich. The slightest excuse triggers conflict, and the poor take over, distributing political power and office at random.

Democratic communities are 'informed by independence and freedom of speech, and everyone has the right to do as he chooses' (VIII, 557b). They breed colourful variety, and are free to experiment with different laws and arrangements according to whim. This may be superficially attractive: it is the blueprint for an 'enjoyable, lax, and variegated kind of political system, which treats everyone as equal, whether or not they are' (VIII, 558c – one almost sees Plato wrinkling his nose here, although in fact no ancient democracy ever approximated to this egalitarian ideal).

Curiously Plato does not go on to detail the evils of this system directly, as he did in the other cases. Perhaps he thinks it is damned obviously enough by the mere fact of its egalitarianism, installing as guides those who know nothing just as readily as those who know their way about. Instead he goes immediately to the parallel in the individual agent, painting a wonderful picture of the disordered, lax, uninhibited hedonistic mind in which each passing fancy is given full rein:

> 'So that's how he lives,' I said. 'He indulges in every passing desire that each day brings. One day he gets drunk at a party, the next day he's sipping water and trying to lose weight; then again, he sometimes takes exercise, sometimes takes things easy without a care in the world, and sometimes he's apparently a student of philosophy. At frequent intervals, he gets involved in community affairs... His lifestyle has no rhyme or reason, but he thinks it enjoyable, free, and enviable and he never dispenses with it.' (VIII, 561c–d)

Well, we have all been there. Again, Plato shows a curious unwillingness to press the issue of just what is wrong or even unhappy about the figure he has painted. His democratic individual sounds a bit like all of us, and a lot like P. G. Wodehouse's delightful Bertie Wooster, a paid-up member of the Drones club, irresolute, weak-willed, rudderless, someone who by his own account 'flits and sips', but potentially attractive enough and certainly happy enough. Why should we side with the iron Victorian aunts who so deplore poor Bertie? Why should steely resolution and rectitude, perfect immunity to the carnival of the appetites, be so admirable? Perhaps in Plato's mind the possibility of a variety of successive desires and appetites is conflated with the internal conflict which destroys harmony and well-being. But if this is so it is a mistake: if I take up the banjo one week and drop it the next, there need be no time at which I suffer any conflict. Overall I will tend to fail in my ambitions, but since by the time I fail they are no longer ambitions, all is well.

Or perhaps such changeability excites his general fear of change and valuation of what is permanent, or perhaps this is just one of those grumpy old men moments.

Plato gets on to firmer ground with the final, most debased form of government: dictatorship. In democracy the overvaluation of freedom naturally degenerates into licence and lawlessness, a process feared in our own times as it was in his, moralized about by innumerable newspaper editors and right-wing commentators. Indeed, Plato's whole description of the process sounds surprisingly modern:

> In these circumstances, for example, teachers are afraid of
> their pupils and curry favour with them, while pupils
> despise their teachers and their attendants as well. In short,
> the younger generation starts to look like the older
> generation, and they turn any conversation or action into a
> trial of strength with their elders; meanwhile, the older

> members of the community adapt themselves to the
> younger ones, ooze frivolity and charm, and model their
> behaviour on that of the young, because they don't want
> to be thought disagreeable tyrants. (VIII, 563a–b)

A world in which democratic leaders like to spend their energy on facelifts, cosmetics and suntans while simultaneously mourning for lost respect would have held no surprises for Plato.

Licence, however, quickly turns to slavery. This happens because the class of 'drones' includes vigorous, criminal natures. These form factions and begin to dominate the democratic assemblies. They silence dissent, and pay off the have-nots with whatever they can steal from those who offend the populace. Dissent and lawsuits break out, heralding the arrival of a demagogue, a self-styled 'champion of the people'. But once such a champion has tasted blood, the road to dictatorship is inevitable and steep. One crime leads to more, practice makes perfect, and the way opens for the Robespierres and Stalins to become our most familiar embodiments of evil and power.

In Books VIII and IX Plato gives a marvellous account of the worms that gnaw at dictatorships: reliance on mercenaries, the resentment of those inevitably victimized on the way to power, the ascendancy of flatterers and suppression of merit, the need to invent foreign enemies, the pervasive atmosphere of fear, and so on. Corresponding to this, the worst form of government, there is the dictatorial personality:

'Oppression and servitude must pervade his mind, with the truly good parts of it being oppressed, and an evil, crazed minority doing the oppressing' (IX, 577d). The fickle appetites and lusts that tyrannize the dictator can never be fulfilled, while his enslavement to them pervades his whole life: 'resentful, unreliable, immoral, friendless, and unjust... he gives room and board to every vice' (IX, 580a).

It is all very squalid, and history shows plenty of examples of tyrants conforming to the picture. We cannot doubt that Plato's loathing of dictatorship was profound and heartfelt. On the other hand, the actual argument is somewhat more flimsy. The question is which psychological type is actually modelled by political dictatorship? On the face of it, one of the dreadful things about a political dictatorship would be the permeating fear. But the libertine that Plato gives us has no particular reason for fear. Plato gives us plenty of reasons for not aspiring to be an actual dictator – the impossibility of friendship as well as the insecurity and fear. But when we get away from politics and back to psychology, the correspondence is at best unclear. One might even ask why the philosopher-king does not model dictatorship, for one part of his mind clearly rules absolutely. They may not be found so often in history, but we can certainly imagine benevolent dictators, or dictators who rule in the firm apprehension of where their subjects' well-being lies. Even among the highly imperfect succession of Roman emperors, some were better than others. Catherine the Great was a learned woman with both friends and lovers, who worked hard for the good of Russia with diligence and constancy.

Plato does not pause over this kind of subtlety. Instead, the drama is that we have a descending order of political systems, and of corresponding personalities. Plato clearly envisaged the degeneration he talks about as a process in time, with democracy nearly the worst and dictatorship the worst and last. He was not familiar with the characteristic processes of our own time whereby in a democracy whoever controls the wealth controls the media, and whoever controls the media controls the ballot – the process that has led us to a new kind of oligarchy. But that is because ancient Athenian democracy was not representative: it was one of direct participation by qualified citizens. The modern twists and turns of the spiral downwards was not so much of a threat.

At the pinnacle is the system, and thence the character, of the philosopher-king, who rules himself and others in the light of his understanding of the good. Below we have mettlesome men, those of mere spirit, and then people in thrall to wealth; these are succeded by the anarchic and irresolute democrat, and worst of all the vicious, friendless dictator, whose power is only a mirror image of his own enslavement to 'terrible desires with prodigious appetites' (IX, 573d).

And with that Socrates finally answers Glaucon's challenge from Book II, of showing that morality, in and of itself and regardless of its consequences, benefits the possessor, and that immorality similarly harms him. Real happiness does coincide with government by virtue and wisdom, the well-ordering of the soul. It is not found either in the pursuit of glory, or of wealth, or in the licence of the democrat, and still less in the slavery hidden behind the unbridled will of the dictator.

To reinforce this message, Plato offers further thoughts, of which the most interesting returns to the threefold division of the mind, now described as the intellectual part directed towards the truth of things, the passionate part directed towards power, success and fame, and the desirous or mercenary part. The philosopher, in whom the first predominates, is then presented as at least acquainted with the pleasures of the other two, while they in turn remain ignorant of the pleasures of philosophy. The point was later repeated by John Stuart Mill in his prim Victorian attempt to show that those who knew both types of pleasure would always choose the 'higher' over the 'lower' – as if philosophers could never enjoy cowboy films or detective stories. The asymmetry, that the philosopher knows a wider spectrum of pleasures, is then transmuted into the philosopher's life being more enjoyable, although the transformation remains something of a conjuring trick. It is very well to talk of the joyous contemplation of the eternal, whether in the shape of mathematics or the form of the good, or God himself, but it is much harder to show that the ecstasy is 'more pleasurable' than, say, that which accompanies the despised pleasures that involve the body. Even saints have been driven to describe their raptures in sexual terms.[2]

Throughout Plato's discussion there is a lurking ambiguity

about the role of the highest part of the mind, the philosophical or intellectual part. Sometimes, it seems that this is the part
that *delivers* knowledge and truth. But more often it is a part
which *values* only knowledge and truth. '[It] is directed at
every moment towards knowing the truth of things, and isn't
interested in the slightest in money and reputation' (IX, 581b).
But these are two very different things. It is one thing to
suggest that we ought to pursue our lives as far as possible *in
the light of* what we know and what we take to be true.
Perhaps that is obvious enough, although one might test it by
wondering whether sometimes illusions are necessary for us
to preserve our sanity. But it is an entirely different thing to
give the *desire* for knowledge and truth a monopoly amongst
human desires, so that in the best form of life it is the only
desire on which the agent acts. Only sleight of hand gets us
from the one, quite ordinary thought, to the other almost
insane thought. For only a little reflection shows that a psychology in which the desire for knowledge and truth is the
only desire is incapable of most of what makes human life rec-
ognizable, let alone enjoyable. Furthermore, it is likely to be
crippled in its own terms, having no compass, for example,
to distinguish between important and unimportant truths,
useful and useless knowledge, and relevant and irrelevant
facts.

This is certainly so if we think of everyday truths, which
may or may not bear upon anything of interest. A trainspotter
may know a lot about the subject of his hobby, and have a
desire, even an obsessive singleminded desire, to know more.

But this hardly puts him at the pinnacle of human virtue and felicity. However, the political discussion so far has been free from the elaborate metaphysics of Books V to VII. That makes its reappearance in a rearguard action at this point. Platonists do not have in mind a life spent in the promiscuous collection of useless and disconnected scraps of truth. They want us to think of a life devoted to Higher Thought, to achieving the wisdom available only to the philosophical elite. Plato argues that because of the superior reality of the objects of this contemplation, by comparison more earthly pleasures are in effect false pleasures, the tinsel and shadows of appearance in place of the solid rock of reality. Some earthly pleasures are necessary, since it is essential to satisfy hunger and thirst. But the rest can and should be ignored. Here the levels of reality established by the Line and the Cave do real work (perhaps real damage), since without them there is no reason for thinking that worldly concerns result only in false pleasures. Pleasures are notoriously fleeting, no sooner enjoyed than lost, but this does not mean that they are not real. It can be pleasurable to watch a cricket match, and even one that lasts five days. It would not be better to watch one that lasted for ever. For one thing, it is integral to the pleasure that the match will have a conclusion.

At this point as well, the original comparison between the sovereign place of philosophy in the soul, and the job of kingship, is stretched beyond breaking point. For philosopher-kings are to rule on behalf of the whole collective: the military and the commercial sectors included. They were to be trustees for the well-ordering and happiness of the whole state. They did not have an agenda of their own which included suppressing or destroying the other classes in the state. They would and could govern the other classes, and this is their proper function, but there is no impression that their government would proceed by telling people that they could not pursue the various jobs to which they were adapted – a policy which would itself trespass against the principle of specialization. Yet by installing the desire for knowledge and truth in its monopoly or near-monopoly position, accompanied only by few 'necessary' desires, Plato induces exactly this bias or distortion in the soul.

We may find Plato's project elevated and sublime, or we may find it self-deceived and fantastical, even before the triumphant calculation that a philosopher's life is 729 times more pleasurable than that of a dictator (IX, 587e). Impressed by the wonderful rhetoric, we may think that Thrasymachus and Glaucon have been answered, that the well-ordered soul is indeed the happiest, and that the injustice or greed, the licentious desires of the immoral person, inevitably fracture and destroy the internal harmony without which happiness is impossible. Or, we may more coolly remember the brutal Athenian envoys, and wonder whether the connection between the injustice they are bent upon, and disharmony within Athens itself, is really so very convincing. But if we think that, then at least Plato will have paved the way for the next thought, which is that a city that could send envoys on such a mission is hardly likely itself to be an earthly paradise. The realpolitik in its foreign affairs will predictably resurface in its internal government, and historically it did. The Athens that sent the Melian envoys was unstable and torn by internal dissent. Nobody can look to today's USA of neo-conservatives as a model of proportion and harmony. Here is Thomas Hobbes's presentation of the decay of the Athenian democracy. This stunning, and chilling, passage was written in 1628, summarizing the account in Thucydides written around 400 BC:

> In those days it was impossible for any man to give good and profitable counsel for the commonwealth, and not incur the displeasure of the people.
>
> For their opinion was such of their own power, and of the facility of achieving whatsoever action they undertook, that such men only swayed the assemblies, and were esteemed wise and good commonwealths men, as did put them upon the most dangerous and desperate enterprizes.
>
> Whereas he that gave them temperate and discreet advice, was thought a coward, or not to understand, or else to malign their power. And no marvel: for much prosperity (to which they had now for many years been accustomed) maketh men in love with themselves; and it is hard for any man to love that counsel which maketh him love himself the less.
>
> And it holdeth much more in a multitude, than in one man. For a man that reasoneth with himself, will not be ashamed to admit of timorous suggestions in his business,

that he may the stronglier provide; but in public deliberations before a multitude, fear (which for the most part adviseth well, though it execute not so) seldom or never sheweth itself or is admitted.

By this means it came to pass amongst the Athenians, who thought they were able to do anything, that wicked men and flatterers drave them headlong into those actions that were to ruin them; and the good men either durst not oppose, or if they did, undid themselves.[3]

Surely it is impossible to read this without reflecting on the parallels in our own time, whether in Washington or London, when the war drums beat and the governments falsify the information, conspire with the proprietors of the press, bully the judiciary, employ known criminals, lie about the results, destroy civil liberties, and of course are deaf to any source of counsel that 'maketh them love themselves the less'.

The evils Hobbes depicts are rather different from those that Plato saw dragging democracy down into dictatorship. But they are equally disorders of the body politic. They infect representative democracy, with its dependency on the ballot box, as badly as they infected the direct democracy of Athens. And they form the most effective riposte to Thrasymachus that exists, thrusting home the point that disorder in pursuit of self-interest, power and licence will be a reflection of internal disorder, of complacency, lack of imagination, rashness and inability to listen to benevolence and prudence, let alone justice.

Book IX ends with more reflections on the state of the virtuous man, and his concern for things of the mind and the harmony of his soul. It is also an explicit statement that the whole thought-experiment has been just that: the presentation of an ideal of life and society, not as a practical proposal, but as a template against which to gauge our own shortcomings:

'If that's what's important to him,' he said, 'he's unlikely to have anything to do with government.'

'Actually,' I said, 'he certainly will, in his own community. But I agree that he probably won't in the country of his birth, short of divine intervention.'

'I see,' he said. 'You mean that he will in the community we've just been founding and describing, which can't be accommodated anywhere in the world, and therefore rests at the level of ideas.'

'It may be, however,' I replied, 'that it is retained in heaven as a paradigm for those who desire to see it and, through seeing it, to return from exile. In fact, it doesn't make the slightest bit of difference whether it exists or will exist anywhere: it's still the only community in whose government he could play a part.'

'Yes, I suppose so,' he said. (IX, 592, a–b)

In many ways this, the end of Book IX marks the climax of *Republic*. Its historical importance is hard to overstate. Of course, many moral traditions – perhaps all – stress moderation, the mastery of desire, the suppression of those aspects that make man the wolf of man, as the key to the well-ordered mind. Plato cannot be singlehandedly credited for all subsequent voicings of that idea. Nor is his idea of renunciation the same as that of the roughly contemporary movement of Buddhism, or the developments of Stoicism some fifty years after Plato's death, and Christianity three centuries later, with their even more insistent otherworldliness, and opposition to desire. On the other hand, the bare truth is that as far as the West is concerned, Plato came first. Other movements of this kind fall into step behind him.

CHAPTER 15

The Exile of the Poets

The same goes for tragic playwrights, then, since they're repre-
senters: they're two generations away from the throne of truth,
and so are all other representers. (X, 597e)

We are less inclined to fall into step behind Plato's attacks on
poetry and painting in the final book. We have already met
the beginning of this battle (in chapters 5 and 7) where Plato
was lamenting first the way in which poets represent the
gods, and secondly the dangers in the poetic habit of taking
the man of spirit or *thumos* as a role model. The point in each
case is that drama, or poetic excellence, is likely to be achieved
by representations of human *weakness*. The calm courage,
justice and wisdom of a Socrates, with his mind on eternal
things, simply does not make for great theatre. In modern
terms, a TV show in which everyone behaves with restraint,
wisdom and dignity, or a Jerry Springer show in which
nobody has anything to confess, and nobody loses their self-
control, is poised to fail. The whole point of such shows is that
they present human folly and weakness for the rest of us to
enjoy.

But on the face of it any such critique cannot apply to all art, and we might share a Platonic distaste for the viler forms of 'entertainment', while remaining proud of our poets and art galleries. But Plato deepens his attack, and makes clear its uncompromising nature, in the final book of *Republic*. Here, he puts the theory of knowledge of the central books to work, using them to show how far away from the truth artistic representation remains.

The precise interpretation of his thought is controversial, and once more even the most sympathetic commentators have despaired.[1] The most straightforward is that it depends on the most 'metaphysical' interpretation of the central books and the metaphor of the Cave. According to that, the domain of truth and knowledge is entirely distinct from the domain of ordinary life. Hence, since the poet or painter only gives us 'representations' of ordinary life, their work is at two removes from reality itself. Actually, taking the allegory of the Cave seriously, representational artists seem to be offering us only shadows of shadows of marionettes, themselves only dimly illuminated copies of the daylight world and its denizens, itself a kind of projection of the light of the sun. By my count, that puts them at least three, and possibly four removes from Truth and Reality. And since being removed from reality is equivalent to being removed from truth and knowledge, poets and painters are incapable of furthering either. They can offer nothing to the well-ordering of the mind.

I doubt if anyone has ever been convinced by this bald argument, depending as it does on the unattractive idea that what the senses show is itself unreal. But it is dependent as well on a more important misunderstanding of what can be represented by poetry or painting. For Plato supposes that representations simply produce secondary *things* – new objects of attention, distinct from and distracting from anything more 'real'. Consider, for example, X, 598b, where Socrates is trying to convince Glaucon of the evils of painting:

'So I want you to consider carefully which of these two alternatives painting is designed for in any and every instance. Is it designed to represent the facts of the real world or appearances? Does it represent appearance or truth?'

'Appearance,' he said.

The disastrous move here is to suppose that representing how something, such as a bed or a chair, or President Bush, appears, is not representing a bed or chair or President Bush at all, but only this different thing, their appearance. This certainly deserves the title of *philosophia perennis*: it is one of the hoariest, most tempting, and most pervasive errors in the entire subject.

For it does not seem to have occurred to Plato that representations may bring out new *aspects* of the very things they represent. We can pursue an interest in the time by looking at a sundial or a watch that represents it. The sundial or watch does not have to *substitute* for an interest in the time. A cartoon of your favourite politician does not just present a substitute or shadow to look at instead of the very person. It presents the person, looking perhaps mad, or bad, or wild or stupid, and it thereby suggests, and potentially reveals, an aspect of the person. Plato makes it sound as though a painting or a poem inevitably substitutes one subject or another. But it does not: the subject stays the same, although what is shown about them may be new. But precisely because of that, art has the capacity to tell us things, just as language does. It is not a distraction from the truth, but potentially an ally of it.

The example of a cartoon is deliberately everyday. But the point is reinforced when we turn to higher artistic exercises. We have already touched on the Romantics' use of Plato, giving us the 'immanent' reading, that first suggested by *Symposium*, of the ascent from the cave. Here is one of the most famous passages, from his great poem 'Lines written a few miles above Tintern Abbey', in which Wordsworth expresses the moral message he finds in nature:

> ... And I have felt
> A presence that disturbs me with the joy
> Of elevated thoughts; a sense sublime
> Of something far more deeply interfused,
> Whose dwelling is the light of setting suns,
> And the round ocean, and the living air,
> And the blue sky, and in the mind of man,
> A motion and a spirit, that impels
> All thinking things, all objects of all thought,
> And rolls through all things. Therefore am I still
> A lover of the meadows and the woods,

And mountains; and of all that we behold
From this green earth; of all the mighty world
Of eye and ear, both what they half-create,
And what perceive; well pleased to recognize
In nature and the language of the sense,
The anchor of my purest thoughts, the nurse,
The guide, the guardian of my heart, and soul
Of all my moral being.[2]

The full poem has many meanings. But what these lines show in particular is the equation between the feelings engendered by the poet's love of the meadows and the woods, and the moral elevation of the awareness they bring to him, of the spirit that rolls through all things, the Wordsworthian equivalent of Plato's Form of the Good. Again, the visible world or 'all the mighty world of eye and ear' reveals an aspect of things, indeed, a highly Platonic aspect of things, an anchor for Wordsworth's entire moral nature. And we in turn, reading the poem, can in principle find it expressing something similar, namely the fact that nature can be revelatory of a Platonic spirit that 'impels all thinking things'. Of course, if we are out of sympathy with Platonic imagery altogether, we may retort that Wordsworth is fantasizing or deceiving himself, but this is hardly an objection that Plato is in a position to make. If Wordsworth is wrong about whether nature reveals something 'far more deeply interfused', then the poem contains a suggestion of falsehood, although even so it might contain a yet more important suggestion of truth, for instance that there is a connection between loving nature and beauty, and loving the good and the true. And if Wordsworth is right the poem contains more than a suggestion of truth. The second possibility must remain open for Platonists. Furthermore, it would be truth put in such a way as to impress and attract an audience, a triumph of education.

Of course, it is not easy to say how art works. Indeed, at that level of generality there may be nothing much to be said about it. Any generalization will meet counter-examples. Indeed, in our receptive and experimental times, it would be almost a duty of the artist to transgress against any attempt at a formula. The only point we need is that sometimes art does work, and work in a revelatory way. It may tell us a new truth about an old subject-matter, or about a new one, about the nature of people or the nature of nature. It may even, if Plato and Wordsworth are right, reveal new truth about the relationship between the world of eye and ear, and the world of morality, or the world of something eternal.

Plato unfortunately intersperses his discussion with jeering remarks, especially about painting, which he seems to think can go on in complete ignorance of its subject-matter, and is in any case confined to attempting *trompe l'œil* imitations of reality. The idea that, for example, a painter like Leonardo da Vinci might need to know a great deal about human anatomy, or one like George Stubbs might first know and then show us an aspect of horses and their lives that had previously been hidden from us, seems completely beyond him.

Given that the most elevated part of the mind is solely interested in knowledge and truth, and that poetry and representational art keep us away from the truth, there is an immediate inference that they pander only to the base part of the mind. They deform even good people (X, 605c). The example Plato gives is of Homer, or any other poet, representing grief, and having the protagonist sing a 'dirge and beat his breast'. And we, the audience, take pleasure in this, surrendering ourselves and sharing 'the hero's pain' (X, 605d). But this all shows the poet satisfying and gratifying the part of ourselves that we ought to pride ourselves on suppressing, and the same goes when other emotions are involved: 'sex, anger, and all the desires and feelings of pleasure and distress which, we're saying, accompany everything we do' (X, 606d). The deformity in question is not just one that might derive from watching murders on television. It is one that might equally come from reading Shakespeare or Wordsworth. Poetic representation:

> irrigates and tends to these things when they should be left
> to wither, and it makes them our rulers when they should be
> our subjects, because otherwise we won't live better and
> happier lives, but quite the opposite. (X, 606d)

There is a significant and sinister change of tack here. The city is no longer one in which the rulers care about the flourishing of *each* of the other parts. The ruling part now claims a *monopoly* of value, indeed, the flourishing of emotion, desire and pleasure is a positive evil, and in the best commonwealth they 'should be left to wither'. This aspect of Plato was enormously influential on the Stoics, who mistrusted emotion in the same exaggerated way, seeing it not merely as something to be governed and moderated and rightly channelled, but as something to be destroyed altogether. It is not just a question of keeping a stiff upper lip, but of stark insensitivity, brutal unfeeling. The ideal man becomes completely impassive, immune to 'desire and feelings of pleasure and distress', no longer a man but a frozen block of ice. This part of Book X does most to justify Nietzsche's charge against Plato of sadism, asceticism and the desire to do the dirt on human life itself. It is also the part that Aristotle most firmly repudiates, integrating reason with the life of the animal, and the proper and necessary role of cultivated and moderate sentiment (although in the final part of his major work, the *Nicomachean Ethics*, Aristotle too succumbs to the idea that the best life is one of pure intellectual contemplation).

At this point we might, in some despair, be tempted to follow the line pursued by the American scholar Leo Strauss, who has been such an influence on modern neo-conservative politics. Strauss had a keen enough eye for the weaknesses in Socrates's overt messages in *Republic*. So he convinced himself that Plato's skill as a dramatist included that of hiding his own teachings, sometimes behind their apparent opposite. It is by the failures of the overt arguments that we learn what we can about justice, politics and the soul. So in the end *Republic* tells us that there is no working analogy between the city and the soul, that Thrasymachus remains victorious, or even that poets are not to be banished.[3] About the only doctrine from Socrates's mouth that remains is that those in government are encouraged to tell noble lies for the good of the state – a convenient exception, of which Strauss's followers appear to have taken full advantage, along with the rehabilitation of Thrasymachus and the superiority of the life of both dictators and plutocrats. We may leave the arguments about this kind of revisionary interpretation to specialists, but since the Straussian Plato is so far away from the figure recognized by everyone else, including Aristotle, who was so close to Plato for so long, it is wise to be sceptical.

CHAPTER 16

The Farewell Myth

> *... the person whose turn was first stepped up and chose the most powerful dictatorship available. His stupidity and greed made him choose this life without inspecting it thoroughly and in sufficient detail, so he didn't notice that it included the fate of eating his own children and committing other horrible crimes.* (X, 619b)

As if anticipating the thought that the monotonous pursuit of the good has by now lost a good deal of its gloss, Plato finishes Book X and *Republic* itself with the charming, and poetic Myth of Er. Here Socrates relaxes the tight condition he has operated under since Glaucon laid down his challenge in Book II. Now, we are permitted to widen our gaze, first to the advantage that almost inevitably attends the well-ordered life on earth, and the disadvantages and punishments that almost inevitably attend the immoral life. Second, on the back of what even a modern sympathizer calls 'one of the few really embarrassingly bad arguments in Plato', Socrates announces the immortality of the soul.[1] Er is a fortunate returnee from the land of the dead. He has told Socrates of the fate of souls in life after death, during the cycles of birth and rebirth. There is the familiar separation of the sheep who go to heaven, and the goats who go below. But there is a twist when, after a thousand years, during which the individual would pay, ten times, a penalty for every crime he had committed during life on earth, the souls are again prepared for another life. The preparation consists of a lottery, run by Necessity and the Fates, determining the order in which they would choose lives. The menu includes examples of each kind of life there is. It is here that the weaknesses of those who are not philosophers come to the fore. Others less fortified will choose worthless lives. Someone stupid and greedy would choose the life of the dictator; others lives of vanity and fleeting honours. Left to themselves, even those who are returning from the heavenly afterlife may choose lives that will lead them to perdition next time round, while those who have been in perdition may sometimes be more cautious. But only the philosopher, the lover of goodness and the repository of wisdom, is equipped to make the right choice in full knowledge of what he is doing.

The thought-experiment is one of choosing lives, and seeing how the different kinds of deformity that have been so carefully depicted during the previous books are adapted to ruining that choice. The lesson survives scepticism about the literal truth of the myth, or about the actual immortality of the soul. We do not have to believe in those in order to appreciate the moral. But, of course, there is still an element of propaganda in the air. As the souls in the parable rummage among possible lives for themselves, the truly good may come across a truly good life, accompanied by the pains and evils that normally attend being bad, compared with a bad life accompanied by the goods that normally accrue only to the upright. This was Glaucon's original worry. Although the message of *Republic* is that they will and should choose the former, we, like Glaucon in Book II, may still remain unconvinced. But for myself I find I am less unconvinced than I had been eight books previously. Some of Socrates's moral grandeur, if not his arguments, must have been at work, patiently, slowly, dissolving the carapaces of self-interest and convention that make up our normal protection in life.

So we finish by reverting to the quotation from Alfred North Whitehead at the beginning. I believe that what we can take from *Republic* is indeed the 'wealth of general ideas' scattered through it. But it is not only that. It is the extraordinary purity of Plato's aim that is overwhelming, his power to pursue one question – how we are to live our lives – through thick and thin, through arguments that might seem fanciful, myths that might seem purely distracting, comparisons that may or may not seem helpful, to circle again and again back to that question. Virginia Woolf expressed the effect of this most powerfully, admittedly citing a different dialogue than *Republic*:

> Are pleasure and good the same? Can virtue be taught? Is virtue knowledge? The tired or feeble mind may easily lapse as the remorseless questioning proceeds; but no one, however weak, can fail, even if he does not learn more from Plato, to love knowledge better. For as the argument mounts from step to step, Protagoras yielding, Socrates pushing on,

what matters is not so much the end we reach as our manner of reaching it. That all can feel – the indomitable honesty, the courage, the love of truth which draw Socrates and us in his wake to the summit where, if we too may stand for a moment, it is to enjoy the greatest felicity of which we are capable.[2]

The confrontation with Thrasymachus, and with Glaucon's challenge, are ones that every age has to make. The Athenian envoys to the Melians are always with us, as are the satisfied images of convention, Polemarchus and Cephalus. We continue to worship men of *thumos* while false pleasure and false goals are the staples of popular entertainment and shape the minds of our children. We have less confidence than Bacon, Pope and Macaulay that the scientific revolution all by itself guarantees pure liberation, and pure progress. At a time when the world's energy resources are disappearing, when many of our cultural resources as they were fashioned in the Enlightenment are similarly felt to be running out, when basing thought on reality is one lifestyle option among others, and is seen by our own statesmen as such, when religious frenzy is counted as virtue, when democracy is sold to plutocracy across the Western world, when politicians openly deride the idea of a public service ethos in the civil service or the other professions, supplanting their higher ranks with placemen and spin-doctors, then our future may well depend on how profoundly we manage to respond to *Republic*.

Introduction

1   G. W. F. Hegel, *Hegel's Philosophy of Right*, translated by T. M. Knox, Oxford, Oxford University Press, 1967.

2   Ralph Waldo Emerson, *Representative Men*, London, John Chapman, 1850, 'Plato'.

3   St Augustine, *City of God*, edited by G. R. Evans, London, Penguin, 2003, Book VIII, Chapter 5, p. 304.

4   The sophists probably never sunk this low, and Plato's aristocratic hostility to them makes him an unreliable witness. Given the nature of Athenian courts and assemblies, learning how to marshal a case was something well worth doing, and if someone could learn how to teach the skill, they deserved their fee. Even in Plato some sophists, such as Protagoras, produce stunning arguments, such as that referred to in note 3 to Chapter 1.

5. Arthur Schopenhauer, 'On Thinking for Yourself', in *Essays and Aphorisms*, edited by R. J. Hollingdale, London, Penguin, 2004, p. 91.

6. Robert Louis Stevenson, 'Talk and Talkers'. in *Essays*, edited by W. L. Phelps, New York, Scribner, 1918. It goes without saying that sound educational practice bears Plato out. I heard that recently a British professor was asked by some dumb

university or government 'management' team what teaching initiatives his department had made in recent years. His reply was that the only way to teach philosophy was discovered by Socrates two thousand years ago, and he had no intention of abandoning it. What Socrates had discovered was the absolute necessity of activities of thought: of sifting, questioning, practising, imagining, reacting. Neither rote learning nor Powerpoint can be more than a beginning to that process.

7. *Phaedrus*, 274d–279c in Plato, *Complete Works*, edited by John Cooper and D. S. Hutcheson, Indianapolis, Hackett, 1997. Dialectic is favourably contrasted with the combative and adversarial practice of argument, 'eristics' at *Republic*, V 454a. I use this edition for other dialogues, but for *Republic* itself I have used Plato, *Republic*, translated by Robin Waterfield, Oxford, Oxford University Press, 1998.

8   It is simplistic to say that Socrates's procedure in the early dialogues, the so-called *elenchus* or method of asking questions but providing no answers, can establish nothing, or nothing 'positive'. It can establish that a theory is inconsistent, or those who hold it are confused, and anything that follows from that.

9   I first heard this point made convincingly by Jonathan Barnes, in Cambridge's Moral Sciences Club.

10 Titles include: A. J. Minnis, *Chaucer and Pagan Antiquity*; E. Bieman, *Plato Baptized; Towards the Interpretation of Spenser's Mimetic Fictions*; Barbara Parker, *Plato's Republic and Shakespeare's Rome*; M. Agar, *Milton and Plato*; G. M. Harper, *The Neoplatonism of William Blake*; J. A. Notopoulos, *The Platonism of Shelley*; J. H. Muirhead, *Coleridge as a Philosopher*. This is only a tiny selection.

11 M. F. Burnyeat, 'Plato as Educator of 19th-century Britain', in

Philosophers on Education, edited by Amélie Oskenberg Rorty, London, Routledge, 1998. I owe the quotations from James Mill and Housman, in the Note on Translations, to this essay.

12 Although the picture is known as *The School of Athens*, this is a name later given to it. Apparently it was originally entitled *Causarum Cognitio*, or knowledge of causes. Certainly the philosophers depicted are not confined to Athens, nor to any of the distinct schools of classical philosophy, such as the Stoics, the Peripatetics, the Cynics, the Sceptics and so on.

13 Coleridge, *Table Talk*, edited by Carl Woodring, London, Routledge, 1990, p. 118, (2 July 1830).

14 Francis Bacon, *The New Organon*, edited by Lisa Jardine and Michael Silverthorne, Cambridge, Cambridge University Press, 2000, Book I, §LXV.

15 Alexander Pope, 'An Essay on Man', in *Poetical Works*, edited by Herbert Davis, Oxford, Oxford University Press, 1978, Epistle II, ll. 23–6.

16 David Hume, 'The Platonist' in *Essays, Moral, Political and Literary*, edited by Eugene Miller, Indianapolis, The Liberty Press, 1987, Part I, Essay XVII.

17 Thomas Babington Macaulay, *Critical and Historical Essays*, London, Longmans Green, 1898, vol. II, 'Lord Bacon'. The metaphor of briars and thistles comes from Bacon, *The New Organon*, op. cit., Book I, §73.

18 Aldous Huxley, *The Perennial Philosophy*, London, Triad Grafton, 1984, p. vii.

19 For Plato and the Victorians, see Richard Jenkyns, *The Victorians and Ancient Greece*, Oxford, Blackwell, 1980, chapter X.

20 Friedrich Nietzsche, *Beyond Good and Evil*, edited by Walter Kaufmann, New York, Random House, 1966, §28.

21 Paul Shorey, *Platonism Ancient and Modern*, Berkeley, Calif., University of California Press, 1938, p. 146.

22 Bertrand Russell, *A History of Western Philosophy*, London, Allen and Unwin, 1946, chapter XV.

Chapter 1

1 Herodotus, *The Histories*, translated by Robin Waterfield, Oxford, Oxford University Press, 1998, Book III, §38, p. 185. I discuss the relativism implicit in this passage in *Being Good*, Oxford, Oxford University Press, 2001, p. 20.

2 John Locke, *An Essay Concerning Human Understanding*, edited by Peter Nidditch, Oxford, Oxford University Press, 1975, Book II, chapter 28.

3 Plato, *Complete Works, Protagoras*, 320d–328d.

4 George Grote, *Plato and the other Companions of Socrates*, London, John Murray, 1865, p. 253. Again, I owe the reference to the essay by M. F. Burnyeat cited in note 11 to the Introduction.

5 Edmund Burke, *Reflections on the Revolution in France*, edited by L. G. Mitchell, Oxford, Oxford University Press, 1999.

6 Aristotle, *De Anima*, edited by W. D. Ross, Oxford, Oxford University Press, 1963, 335. I owe the reference to work by James Murphy.

Chapter 2

1 Thucydides, *The Peloponnesian War*, translated by Rex Warner, London, Penguin, 1954, pp. 400–408.

2 There was an English edition earlier than Hobbes, but it was translated from French.

3 David Hume, *A Treatise of Human Nature* (1888), edited by

Selby-Bigge, Oxford, Oxford University Press, 1978, p. 620.

4   *Henry IV Part I*, Act V, scene 1, l. 133.

5   There has been some debate over Thucydides's motive in presenting the dialogue so starkly. One line advanced even in antiquity is that, since he had by then been exiled by them, he simply wanted to present the Athenians as gangsters or pirates. A different line places it in the context of Athens's catastrophic Sicilian expedition, seeing Thucydides as illustrating the arrogance of imperial power to readers who know that pride comes before a fall. Another line sees it as presenting an example of a universal trait, the tendency to act badly out of fear. This thought becomes prominent in Hobbes.

6   Friedrich Nietzsche, *The Genealogy of Morals*, edited by W. D. Ross, Oxford, Oxford University Press, 1963, Book II.

Chapter 3

1   David Hume, *Enquiry Concerning the Principles of Morals*, edited by Tom Beauchamp, Oxford, Oxford University Press, 2002, section IX, para 22.

Chapter 4

1   Richard Crossman, *Plato Today*, London, George Allen and Unwin, 1937; Sir Karl Popper, *The Open Society and its Enemies*, London, Routledge, Kegan and Paul, 1945, vol. 1, *Plato*.

Chapter 5

1   Not only do studies seem to give different results, but meta-studies, that is, studies of what actual studies have shown, give different results as well.

2   Scientifically minded readers may be reminded of the

discovery of so-called 'mirror neurons' in the frontal lobes of primates, thought to be involved in our ability to read the minds of others, empathize with each other, and learn languages.

3 Plato, *Complete Works, Ion,* 534.

4 Maurice Cranston, *The Romantic Movement,* Oxford, Blackwell, p. 88.

Chapter 6

1 Sir Karl Popper, *The Open Society and its Enemies,* vol. I, *Plato,* p. 105.

2 See also Callicles's tremendous speech in *Complete Works, Gorgias,* 482d–487.

3 For illuminating comment on Freud's expansion of the view, see Jonathan Lear, *Freud,* London, Routledge, 2005, p. 24ff.

Chapter 7

1 Hume, *A Treatise of Human Nature,* Book II, Part 3, section 3, p. 415.

2 This section owes a great deal to the superb treatment in Angela Hobbs, *Plato and the Hero,* Cambridge, Cambridge University Press, 2000.

3 Kenneth Clark, *Ruskin Today,* London, John Murray, 1964, p. 269.

4 Aristotle, *On Rhetoric,* translated by George Kennedy, Oxford, Oxford University Press, 1991, 1389a3–b13. The passage is quoted in Hobbs, op. cit., p. 40.

5 See, for example, *The Gay Science,* translated by George Kaufmann, New York, Random House, 1974, 349.

Chapter 8

1 Henry Sidgwick, *The Methods of Ethics*, London, Macmillan, 1874.

2 Charles Kahn, 'George Grote's *Plato and the Companions of Sokrates*' in *George Grote Reconsidered*, edited by W. M. Calder and S. Trzaskoma, Hildenheim, Weidmann, 1996, p. 49.

Chapter 9

1 See R. M. Ogilvie, *Latin and Greek, a History of the Influence of the Classics on English Life from 1600 to 1918*, London, Routledge, 1964. See also John Glucker, 'Plato in England, the Nineteenth Century and After', in *Utopie und Tradition*, edited by H. Funke, Würzburg, Könighausen u. Neumann, 1987.

2 Nietzsche, *Beyond Good and Evil*, op. cit., p. 3.

3 Immanuel Kant, *Critique of Pure Reason*, translated by Norman Kemp Smith, London, Macmillan, 1929, Introduction, A5/B9, p. 47.

Chapter 10

1 For an excellent modern treatment, see A. D. Smith *The Problem of Perception*, London, Harvard University Press, 2002.

Chapter 11

1 St Augustine, *City of God*, op. cit., Book VIII, chapter 4.

2 Arnobius, *Against the Pagans*, translated by Michael Chase, Chicago, University of Chicago Press, 1993, quoted in Pierre Hadot, *Plotinus or The Simplicity of Vision*, p. 24.

3 The classic history of this theme is A. O. Lovejoy, *The Great Chain of Being*, Cambridge, Mass., Harvard University Press, 1936.

4 The relation between 'anamnesis' or the doctrine of recollection in Plato, and the inner light of the Cambridge Platonists, is sensitively explored by Dominic Scott, in 'Reason, Recollection and the Cambridge Platonists', in *Platonism and the English Imagination*, edited by Anna Baldwin and Sarah Hutton, Cambridge, Cambridge University Press, 1994, pp. 139–50. For Wordsworth and Coleridge, articles by Keith Cunliffe and Anthony Price in the same volume have been invaluable.

5 The phrase is from Shelley's lament for the dead Keats, *Adonais*, §54, in Percy Bysshe Shelley, *The Major Works*, edited by Zachary Leader and Michaël O' Neill, Oxford, Oxford University Press, 2003.

Chapter 12

1 I am particularly indebted here to the excellent discussion in Melissa Lane's remarkable book, *Plato's Progeny*, London, Duckworth, 2001.

Chapter 13

1 Andrea Wilson Nightingale, *Spectacles of Truth in Classical Greek Philosophy*, Cambridge, Cambridge University Press, 2006.

2 Francis Bacon, *The New Organon*, op. cit. Book 1, xcv.

3 Waterfield has an especially illuminating note on the problem, in the Oxford translation; see Introduction, note 7.

4 The most extended modern discussion is *Invariances* by Robert Nozick, Cambridge, Mass., Harvard University Press, 2001.

Chapter 14

1 Plato is rather down on drones, presumably through not knowing the biology of the honey bee, *apis mellifera*. He thinks

of drones as the 'bane of the hive' and at VIII, 552c he divides them into two kinds, one of which is harmless, but the other of which has a sting (and is to represent the criminal class). In fact, drones are not the bane of the hive but are vital to it, since they alone can fertilize the queen, dying as a result, and all drones are stingless.

2 I discuss the splendid case of St Teresa of Avila, in *Lust*, New York, Oxford University Press, 2004, pp. 25–6.

Chapter 15

1 A fine recent discussion is in Julia Annas, *An Introduction to Plato's Republic*, Oxford, Oxford University Press, 1981, pp. 336–44.

2 William Wordsworth, 'Lines written a few miles above Tintern Abbey' (1798), *Lyrical Ballads*, edited by W. G. B. Owen, Oxford, Oxford University Press, 1969.

3 Leo Strauss, *The City and Man*, Chicago, University of Chicago Press, 1964, Part II, 'Plato's Republic'.

Chapter 16

1 Annas, *Introduction to Plato's Republic*, op. cit., p. 345.

2 Virginia Woolf, 'On Not Knowing Greek', in *The Common Reader, London*, Hogarth Press, 1925.

FURTHER READING

Many books and papers have helped me as well as those already listed. The best students' guide to the work is Nikolas Pappas, *Guidebook to Plato and the Republic* (London, Routledge, 1995). Julia Annas, *An Introduction to Plato's Republic* (Oxford, Oxford University Press, 1981), is a classic modern discussion combining philosophical depth with readability to a remarkable degree. Sir Karl Popper, *The Open Society and its Enemies* (London, Routledge, Kegan and Paul, 1945), vol. I, *Plato*, is a polemical masterpiece, and as one-sided as that implies. Melissa Lane's treatment of the modern reception of Plato in *Plato's Progeny* (London, Duckworth, 2001), often left me worried whether there was anything left to say. An older classic, Paul Shorey's *Platonism Ancient and Modern* (Berkeley, University of California Press, 1938), is a wonderfully urbane and learned ramble through historical byways.

and philosopher-kings 23, 86
in *Republic* 15–16, 53–8
and specialization 70–1
Pope, Alexander 11, 161
Popper, Karl 54–5, 56, 69–70
Porphyry 8, 106
property ownership 57, 68
proportion, and harmony 78, 110,
114, 119, 145
Protestantism, and Plato 109
purity, and integrity 61–2, 65–7
Pythagoras 10, 98–9, 119, 121–2,
124

Quine, W. V. O. 28

Raphael (Raffaeo Sanzio), *The School of Athens* 9
rationalism, and empiricism 14,
123
reality:
and artistic representation
59–62, 65, 149–52, 154–5
and belief 90–2
and shadows 13, 99–102, 104,
143, 150–2
ultimate 13–15, 95–7, 105–6, 110
worldly 9–13, 15, 64, 110–11, 113
reason:
analogy with ruling elites 50–1
and desire and spirit 50–1, 73,
82–4, 88–9, 156
and divine inspiration 64
and ends 88–9

and illumination 97–8, 108
and morality 27–30, 82–4
recollection, and innate knowledge
109
relativism, and change 126–7
religion *see* Christianity; transcendentalism
Republic:
analogy of communities and
individuals 47–58
and artists 57, 59–67, 149–57
date of writing 22
and dialectic 7
and gender equality 57, 79
and ideal state 47–58
importance 7–20
length 15
and politics 15–16, 53–8
portrayal of Socrates 16–17
and reality 12–13
revisionist views 156–7
theory of knowledge 13, 16
as thought-experiment 49–50,
54–5, 147, 159–60
translations ix–x
see also morality
reputation, and convention 24, 35,
38, 44, 45, 73
rewards of morality 39–40, 44–5
Richards, I. A. x
Ring of Gyges 42–6
Roman Catholicism, and Aristotle
108–9
Romanticism, and art 63, 66, 152

Index compiled by Meg Davies (Registered Indexer, Society of Indexers)